A WRITER'S SPACE

Make Room to Dream, to Work, to Write

ERIC MAISEL, PH.D.

adamsmedia

Avon, Massachusetts

Published by
Adams Media, an F+W Publications Company
57 Littlefield Street, Avon, MA 02322. U.S.A.
www.adamsmedia.com

ISBN-10: 1-59869-460-X
ISBN-13: 978-1-59869-460-4

Printed in the United States of America.

J I H G F E D C B A

Library of Congress Cataloging-in-Publication Data
is available from the publisher.

This publication is designed to provide accurate and authoritative information with regard to the subject matter covered. It is sold with the understanding that the publisher is not engaged in rendering legal, accounting, or other professional advice. If legal advice or other expert assistance is required, the services of a competent professional person should be sought.
—From a *Declaration of Principles* jointly adopted by a Committee of the American Bar Association and a Committee of Publishers and Associations

Many of the designations used by manufacturers and sellers to distinguish their product are claimed as trademarks. Where those designations appear in this book and Adams Media was aware of a trademark claim, the designations have been printed with initial capital letters.

Interior illustration by Grant Hanna.

This book is available at quantity discounts for bulk purchases.
For information, please call 1-800-289-0963.

For Ann,
Who for thirty years has provided the right space

CONTENTS

I. PHYSICAL SPACE

II. HOME SPACE

III. MIND SPACE

IV. EMOTIONAL SPACE

V. REFLECTIVE SPACE

VI. IMAGINED SPACE

CONTENTS

VII. PUBLIC SPACE

VIII. EXISTENTIAL SPACE

IX. EPILOGUE: CREATIVE SPACE: A WRITING FABLE

PART I

Physical Space

CHAPTER 1

Thinking about Your Writing Space

Other books for writers will tell you where to insert the commas and why your Parisian character shouldn't wear a beret unless he's Basque. I want to chat with you about some other things: how to get into the right "space" to write, how to orient and organize your neurons, how to sanctify and enliven your physical space, and how to create imagined spaces in which magic can happen.

In the thirty-six chapters that compose this book I'll use the metaphor of "space" to communicate how you can get a grip on your writing life and transform yourself from an occasional writer to a regular writer. My job, as I see it, is to cheerlead, to whip you into a frenzy, and once in a while to make you smile. Naturally, you will have to do the actual work.

Let's begin with your physical space, the place where you write. Should your desk face the door? Should it face the wall?

3

What if your right shoulder faces the door and your desk is slightly to the north of the room's only window? Should you keep books in your room or are they in league with the devil? Should your computer be stripped of its e-mail capabilities and of any software that can produce a game of solitaire? Should you wear pajamas or a business suit? Should you keep a second office in one of those urban writing centers (some with a two-year waiting list) where you go to really write? Should your walls be Navajo white, cream-colored, or Chinese red? Should your chair swivel? Should your head?

Are these the right questions?

Think of a hospital operating room. You wouldn't want your surgeon distracted by the view, would you? If that operating room overlooked the ocean, you would hope that someone would have the good sense to pull the curtains, so as to prevent glare and a roving eye. Amy Tan, for instance, explained that she writes in a "very womblike place." She has two offices, one in New York and one in San Francisco. The one in New York is a former closet with low ceilings and her office in San Francisco has a window she keeps covered with drapes to block out the view. "I cannot deal with distractions," she confessed. "I had a beautiful office with views of the Golden Gate Bridge and the Bay but my assistant, Ellen, has that office now."

Like a surgeon, your goal is to focus. You want to muster your resources and canalize your energy. As a general rule a large space dissipates energy, noise produces distraction, views rob the mind of neurons, toys cry out to be played with, and even a book near at hand is a reason to stop early. Of course you are permitted messes, piles of papers, shelves of books, iconic snow globes and photographs, and a view of the garden. However, your goal is to canalize your energy and have your brain connect to your fingers in such a seamless way that words appear on your computer screen by magic. For this to happen, your best bet is simplicity: a little quiet, a little organization, and a little reverence.

Maybe church is a better analogy than an operating room.

You will do better work with a quiet room, a closed door, a serene view or no view at all, a little organization (and all the mess you like), and that feeling in your heart that you are in the only church you need, the one where you pray poems and praise prose. What does a church need? Does it really need all that Gothic grandiosity or ornate rococo cake decoration? Or does it need just a bench, silence, and a little awe? That is all your writing space needs: a chair, a table, silence, and a little awe. Add anything else you like, if it serves you; but don't forget this simple ideal.

You also want the kind of organization that allows you to move as fluidly as you can from idea to idea, from chapter to chapter, from file to file, from story to story, from heartbeat to heartbeat. An extreme example of this organizational nicety was Isaac Asimov's. He attributed the fact that he was able to write 500 books during his career to the way he set up his office—with tables all around the perimeter, each with several typewriters on it. Each typewriter stood ready for a different project and he would just "work my way around the room." You need not go this far, but you do need to know where to reach when you are looking for Chapter 3 or those notes for that essay on Byzantium.

Everything—the wallpaper, the cobwebs, the size of your font—is for the sake of your current project. You want to be reminded of and enveloped by that rich, new project, not by some past disaster (or success) or some future vibration. Alice Hoffman, for instance, paints her office a different color every time she starts a new book, one that resonates with the book's themes, and sets out items that remind her of that book. You are a serially monogamous writer, in love with this precious new thing: let your space show it.

That great Greenwich Village character Joe Gould, portrayed in a famous Alice Neel painting with three penises, wrote seven million words in his crazy career as an oral historian and street person. He accomplished this prodigious feat without ever having a home writing space or even a home. He wrote on park benches, under awnings during rainstorms, sitting on the curb, and, of course, in cafés, where sometimes he was hired by the café proprietor at the cost of a cup of coffee and a pastry to write and "look Bohemian." Unfortunately, they were seven million words of psychotic ramblings. Might he have done better work with a quiet room of his own (and some mental health)? I think so.

You want a quiet room (and some mental health). You may also write in airports, in Paris, on top of a mountain, at the laundry, and with Beethoven blaring. You will of course want to write whenever it strikes you to write, wherever you happen to be, and whether you have your best pen with you or only your purple lipstick. But let us agree on this basic proposition: chair, table, closed door, a computer or a pad, a little awe, a little love, maybe the shades drawn, and your brain humming. That is your physical space, and your church service.

LESSON 1

Moving words from your brain to the page is a prolonged act of thinking and feeling that requires that you inhabit a physical space. Any given physical space will do a better or poorer job of serving this process: how good a job does yours do?

To Do

1. Assess your current physical space. Is it quiet (or at a noise level that you like)? Is it secluded (or open in a way that you prefer)? Is

it organized (or disorganized in an "organized" way)? Is it calming (or energizing in a way that suits you)? Is it the way you want it and need it to be?

2. Describe your ideal writing space. What can you do to transform your current space so that it more resembles your ideal space?

3. What is the biggest problem with your current space? Identify three possible solutions, decide which is the most feasible to implement, and make those changes.

4. Is your space private? If it isn't, can you make it more private or even completely private?

- maybe some soft places

Biggest problem:
    Share with art space
      ① another place just for writing
    →② clean away art every time
      ③

CHAPTER 2

Picking Your Space

Often the places that are available to us do not suit us simply because we are not inclined to write. One client, an American poet living in Amsterdam with his Dutch wife and their two daughters, could not write in his perfectly fine study because the silence was just slightly off, his chair was slightly ill-fitting, his desk was slightly at the wrong height, and his door, as it didn't lock, was often opened. The very threat of that door opening stopped him from writing. He knew that he was being "neurotic" about all this, but he nevertheless clung to his certainty that his space was just not conducive to writing. So he didn't write.

Of course his physical space wasn't the issue—nor is physical space likely to be the issue with you. For example, a client of mine took one large step after another in order to position herself to write her book. She gave up her lucrative, sixty-hour-a-week day job. She convinced her husband that they should move to a rural area where the quiet would be conducive to thinking and writing. They moved to a rugged, beautiful area, purchased a house with stunning views, and reinvented themselves, he as a consultant, she as an online content writer for Web sites. They loved their new life, they loved the fact that deer visited and that storms whipped through the valley. But she didn't begin her book.

Every morning she came into her study, with its stupendous views through floor-to-ceiling windows, and felt a kind of paralysis. So as to be doing something, she'd check her e-mail, attend to business, and keep busy hour after hour until it was time to take a walk in nature or have lunch with her husband. The morning would pass this way, efficiently, productively, and sadly. The afternoon would prove even harder—more work accomplished, more sadness, more hours spent not writing her book.

She could perfectly attribute her paralysis. Her parents had criticized her. She didn't feel confident. She hadn't written a book before. She wasn't certain what the book was supposed to be about. She found her writing workmanlike but not sizzling. Her husband was a little needy and distracted her with his presence. She had to do her online writing to make money. Part of her found her book not important enough to write. Another part of her found her book not interesting enough to write. She got headaches easily. She'd never gotten her two short stories published, which was demoralizing. People loved her writing but their praise seemed unearned and so she dismissed it—even turned it into criticism. Her paralysis made perfect sense. She had the list to prove it.

I learned all this and more in our first session. It came my turn to speak. I told her that I understood. I told her that she was making only one mistake. The mistake she was making was to think that she was writing a book. I told her that the word "book" had the iconic, mesmerizing power to snuff out the possibility of writing. She was inadvertently picturing her book among other books like *War and Peace* and *Crime and Punishment*, books that overwhelmed her and made her feel small and incapable. I told her that it was a big mistake to think that she was writing a book. In fact, what she was writing was a draft. The book would come later—perhaps much later—after countless pratfalls. She had no book to write, only a draft. Did she understand that effort and not excellence was the issue? She nodded telephonically.

She agreed that she knew what she needed to do: the work. And indeed she tried. But the startling vista that confronted her in her study, a vista so large and engaging that even if you turned your back on it you felt its presence and its immensity, hurt rather than helped her. The floor-to-ceiling windows, devoid of covering, let in too much distraction. She tried moving her chair, moving her desk, averting her eyes, but nothing worked. Finally she decided to poke about the house and look for another workspace. She came upon a small, windowless room, not much larger than a walk-in closet, stepped inside it, and felt right silence descend instantly. This became her writing space, the place where she actually wrote. Finally she began her novel.

Once you internally agree to get your work done you can write almost anywhere, but that doesn't mean that you can vanish into your writing as easily in one environment as in another. In our first small house, I had a windowless basement study that was perfect for me. In our next house, a big suburban one, I had a score of objectively excellent writing spots and none of them felt congenial. In the upscale city apartment that followed that house, we had panoramic views that proved paralyzing. In our current small Edwardian flat, a room at either end suits me splendidly, the room at the eastern end bright in the morning, the room at the western end bright in the afternoon.

Clearly these are subjective matters. In her excellent writers' companion *The Writer's Mentor*, Cathleen Rountree explained: "Poet and novelist Sherman Alexie, author of *Indian Killer* and *Smoke Signals*, does much of his writing at 3 A.M. at an International House of Pancakes. Eudora Welty said that she straight-pinned pieces of her stories together on the dining room table, as though she were pinning together parts of a dress." Barbara

Sjoholm explained in *Incognito Street*: "I knew, the first morning that I woke up in Hamar [in Norway], in my room in the big wooden house that looked just like something out of a Carl Larsson painting, that I was exactly in the right place. The walls were wainscoted with painted blue gray wood, the room had a single wooden bed and, most important, there was a pine table in front of the window, a table for writing."

Which spot in your house will be your primary writing space? Get up and start your investigations. Give every reasonable spot a try—and every unreasonable spot, too.

LESSON 2

Some writing spots are more congenial than other writing spots. Find your best spot; or create it, if it doesn't exist, by pushing furniture around, by reclaiming the junk room, by doing whatever is necessary.

To Do

1. Be willing to write. No writing space will serve you if you aren't.
2. Go on a vision quest and locate the place in your home where you will write.
3. Test out your writing space by writing in it.
4. Keep writing there.

CHAPTER 3

Protecting Your Space

Your husband comes home. You chat with him, have a drink together, have dinner. Then you go to your writing space, close the door, boot up your computer, empty your mind, and ready yourself to continue your novel.

Right about the time the desktop icons appear on your computer screen, your husband storms into your study to complain about the auto insurance premiums. Don't you agree that it's time to switch to another company? Out of politeness, you listen to him vent about the price of insurance, the price of gas, and the price of his favorite cereal. You've heard this rant so often that you can repeat it word for word; you grit your teeth and wait for the rant to end.

When he's finally done, you turn to your computer screen and discover that you are entirely in the wrong frame of mind to write. You are angry with your husband, angry with yourself, frustrated about how long it's taking you to write this novel, and suddenly exhausted. You turn off the computer and go to bed.

You didn't protect your writing space very well, did you?

It's six-thirty in the morning. You're at your computer, half-ready to write, but you decide to check your e-mail one more time (you checked it already first thing, five minutes previously). A mildly interesting, mildly important e-mail has arrived about an event benefiting a cause you support. You could wait to deal with it—but you decide to deal with it right away.

You craft your reply, which takes twenty minutes. You decide to whom you want to forward the message, then realize that you had better send a little explanation along with the forwarded e-mail. That takes another hour. Now you're hungry, and more e-mails have come in, and you planned only to write from six-thirty till eight, as you have many other things to do. So you make a date with yourself to write at four P.M. You answer a few new e-mails, get up from the computer at nine, and compliment yourself on three productive hours at your desk.

You didn't protect your writing space very well, did you?

The power company is digging up the street in front of your house, which is where your study is located. You sit there in front of your computer and can't write a word as heavy machinery rumbles up and down the street and men with jackhammers crack through the pavement. You feel proud that you aren't running out of the room screaming, but you can't get a lick of work done.

Of course, you could move to the back of the house, where it is relatively quiet, which would take you about a minute to do, as your computer is a laptop and completely portable. It even has a charged battery. But you don't write in the back of the house; you only write in your study. So you sit there, fuming, your head throbbing, and after another few agonizing minutes you throw in the towel and shut down your computer.

You didn't protect your writing space very well, did you?

Your in-laws are visiting. You could go to your study or you could sit with them over breakfast. You've already had nine consecutive meals with them and there isn't a thing left to chat about, except perhaps the things you disagree about, but you choose to sit with them.

You make them their dry toast and put out the orange marmalade and mutter, "I thought I might get a little writing done this morning." Your mother-in-law exclaims, "By all means!" which you take to mean that she's as sick of you as you are of her. But you hear yourself say, "Oh, no, that's okay. I'll join you for breakfast." You bring your slice of toast to the table and the small talk begins.

You didn't protect your writing space very well, did you?

Your days are full and you only have two hours in the evening in which to write. Your teenage daughter, whom you love, is learning Italian and wants to practice with you. You don't mind this because you have your heart set on a trip to Italy and want to know how to do more than order espresso and find the bathroom. So you practice Italian with her.

This is pleasant and even a blessing. But no writing gets done. You'd like to stop the practicing, but you don't know how to get out of it without disappointing your daughter. So you keep practicing. One day you discover that you can order a complete meal in Italian, but your novel is no closer to being finished.

You didn't protect your writing space very well, did you?

What should you have done?

Scenario 1: Locked the door. Or said to your husband, "Dear, I'm working now. But I'll be happy to discuss the insurance in about an hour."

Scenario 2: Skipped dealing with that "important" e-mail, which you could have dealt with in the evening.

Scenario 3: Moved to the back of the house, even though you "don't write there."

Scenario 4: Let them eat breakfast while you got a little writing done.

Scenario 5: Said to your daughter, "This has been ever so pleasant! Now I need to get back to my novel."

You are the only one who can protect you writing space. To protect it you may have to enlist the aid of your family. You may have to let your husband know when the insurance chats will occur, inform your children that you are completely available to them except for those two hours each evening when you are utterly unavailable, and explain to your in-laws that their visit is an amazing blessing but that you also intend to get some writing done. You may have to protect it by moving it to another part of the house. You may have to protect it with soundproofing, with Do Not Enter signs, and with a lock that locks you in it. You are the only one who can protect it: you are the warden, prison guard, and convict.

LESSON 3

Your writing space is a literal space and it's also a metaphoric space. Both need protection, the first with explicit rules, the second with strong intentions.

To Do

1. Write out your security pledge: how you will protect your writing space.
2. Have a chat with anyone who currently invades your writing space and spell out your new ground rules.
3. Protect your writing space with a talisman, amulet, icon, or shotgun.
4. Write a little, safe and snug in your protected space.

I will set time apart for email –
not check compulsively.
I will do other work later in
the day.

CHAPTER 4

Honoring Your Space

J t matters what you do when you are in your writing space. It matters whether you are working on your novel or surfing the Internet. It matters whether you are pining for the one agent who will fall in love with your writing or preparing to query thirty agents. It matters whether you are building your platform by offering to write columns, speak at churches, and lead teleseminars or whether you are fantasizing about who will play the lead when your novel is made into a movie. Just sitting in your space isn't enough; it matters what you do there.

It matters whether you are writing your second novel, even though your first one hasn't sold yet, or brooding that you aren't published. It matters whether you are writing an e-mail to your literary agent, with whom you haven't been in contact for six months, or waiting for the phone to ring with news that she's sold your novel. It matters whether you are honorably revising your novel, maybe for the fifth time, because it's still muddled in spots, or doing everything you can to avoid its muddles. It matters what you are doing.

It matters whether you are contemplating some shortcut—maybe stealing a few scenes from that first novel of yours that went awry and dropping them into your current novel, where they might just possibly fit—or sitting up straight in your chair and writing the scenes your novel needs. It matters whether you are thinking of hiring an editor, a ghostwriter, or even the handyman to write your book, because you are completely sick of it and can't face it, or whether you are biting the bullet, brewing some tea, and hunkering down to write.

It matters whether you are sitting in the dark with the shades drawn and your computer off, because you are sad and depressed, or whether you are helping yourself out of your depression by whatever means possible. If that means getting out of the house, that's what it means; better that than sitting in your writing space inert and morose.

Honoring your writing space means that if you are embroiled in tasks, dramas, crises, and errands, you ring a bell at your appointed time and let all of that go. You enter your writing space clear-headed and unencumbered. If you are tired from your day job, you splash water on your face; if you are exhausted from your mate's chatting, you take an aspirin and a quick nap; if you have a hundred things to do before you get to write, you put that long list aside and remind yourself what honor means.

Honoring your writing space means that if you need to read what you've previously written, you read it. If you need to plunge forward without rereading, you plunge forward. You accept that you have craft to master, attention to pay, and a routine to follow. You refuse to attribute any of your shortcomings to your "artistic nature." You get off your high horse and sit right down on your swivel chair, do the work, and honor the process.

At the same time, you set the bar sufficiently high. It is fine to write articles; but is it fine to never write a book? It is fine to begin your thirtieth journal; but is it fine to have written only journal entries? It may seem funny to get off your high horse and also set the bar high, but the two go together beautifully: you agree to work without fanfare and you choose work equal to your dreams.

You honor your writing space by recovering, if you are an addict. You honor your writing space by becoming an anxiety expert, a real pro at mindfulness and personal calming. You honor your writing space by affirming that you matter, that your writing life matters, and that your current writing project matters.

You honor your writing space by entering it with this mantra: "I am ready to work." You enter, grow quiet, and vanish into your writing.

Honor is a funny word, a loaded word, a difficult word. It is not a word to toss around lightly. But I'm willing to bet that you place it at the very top of your list of words with personal meaning. I bet you love it, believe in it, and aspire to it. Live that way, then! Honor the fact that you believe in honor and construct your writing life around it.

If you live your life as you intend it to be lived, you will find yourself in your writing space thousands of times. Sixty years of writing, two hours a day, translates to better than 50,000 hours in your writing space. Squander some of those hours—we all must. Indulge a bad mood for some of those hours—we all do. Write poorly during some of those hours—there's no way around that. But try your best to honor your writing space. That's the key intention.

LESSON 4

It matters what you do in your writing space. Do the right things.

To Do

1. Make a list of the things you will never do in your writing space. Keep that list handy, right beside your computer.
2. Make a list of the things you will only occasionally do in your writing space. Keep that list handy, right beside your computer.
3. Make a list of the things you intend to do most of the time that you are in your writing space. Keep that list handy, right beside your computer.
4. Consolidate these three lists into one; then mind it.

CHAPTER 5

Adding Spaces

Sometimes you want to be silent in your room with your door closed. Sometimes you want to be silent among people as you sit in a café. Sometimes you want an ascetic, crystalline experience with snow in the air and a view of a Norwegian fjord (or at least a view of a poster of a fjord). Sometimes you want a humid, intense experience, with thousands of people passing below your window day and night (or its rough equivalent, a sidewalk table on a hot summer night). You have your laptop computer: the whole world is your office, if you will let it be.

There are so many splendid places where you might find yourself writing! You might find yourself in your own garden. You might find yourself in a bookstore café, on a bench by the lake, or in the newly refurbished library around the corner. You might find yourself moving with the laptop around your house, now upstairs, now downstairs, now out on the front steps to catch a few rays of sunshine. You might find yourself in an Italian bakery, a Swedish sandwich shop, a Russian deli. Your mind was always portable; so was your pad and pen; and now your computer is also. What fun!

It is a bad trick of the mind to announce to yourself that you can only write in a certain place, in certain circumstances, in a certain kind of weather, at a certain time of the day, after having a certain kind of meal, with a certain sort of pen. It is fine to have preferences but important to commit to writing anywhere. That way you can grab ideas when you're away from home; you can take a little writing trip when you feel dull at your desk; you can choose among your excellent haunts and decide which feels most congenial at the moment. By all means maintain a primary writing place; then add alternates.

When I go out to write, I go to a particular café a short walk away. I could go to other cafés, but this one is congenial. I usually stay for no more than an hour, as after an hour I crave a second pastry. If I want to stay out a bit longer and the weather is decent, I sit on one of the benches along our main street: there is a bench in front of the supermarket, a bench in front of the community center, a bench in front of the video store, and a bench in front of a hair salon. I choose my writing bench according to how much sun it is getting: the bench in front of the supermarket rarely gets the sun and rarely gets my business.

I wish I could sit on a bench in the children's playground behind the library, but, for safety reasons, adults aren't allowed unless accompanied by children. I wish I could sit in the wine bar but it is a little too small and intimate, a little too hard not to chat with the proprietress, who has good stories about her time in Rome. I wish I could sit in the deli, but sandwiches are my downfall and the lamb-in-pita cries out to me with a plaintive wail. I wish I could sit in the library, but it reminds me of the prison of elementary school. But I am blessed with enough writing haunts and I do not mourn these losses.

And if I wanted to hop in the car, how many splendid places I could add! There are a dozen congenial cafés along just one stretch of Valencia Street, a neighborhood thoroughfare not five minutes' drive from here. I could go to museums and sit in their cafés; I could sit on college campuses; I could mingle with tourists; I could spend the day out on the town with my laptop. I can hear the zipper now as I undo its Chinese red carrying case and pull the laptop out. Maybe I am having an Irish coffee; maybe I am sitting on a bench atop Bernal Hill, with its stunning views of San Francisco; wherever I find myself, that is a writing space.

Go on a vision quest this week and find some congenial spots to write. Bring your laptop or your pad and make sure that the spots really work. Set yourself a special writing goal for the week and meet it in a variety of writing haunts, proving to yourself that it is possible to write unselfconsciously in the world. Make a list of your new writing haunts and maybe even a map, something like a treasure map. A writer's space is wherever she lands; her treasure is the writing she gets done in these myriad spots.

Be open and inventive. Use your dining room table to spread out the table of contents of your novel, one chapter title per index card, so that you can rearrange chapters effortlessly. Use your neighborhood Starbucks as the place you go when you want to create the marketing plan for your new book, a task of so little interest that you need a place built for breaks. Use the waiting room of your dentist's office to make notes for an article, the side of the road to jot down the last line of your poem that just came to you. Stand ready!

How many haunts do you need? Maybe only that primary one: that sofa by the window bathed in light and silence, that desk in the study, that kitchen table with its bowls of nuts and candies. But you'll probably want an alternate space, too, a space that serves as a treat, as a destination, and to help break up your routine. By actually using your alternate space you remind yourself that you can—and should—write anywhere.

LESSON 5

In addition to your primary writing space, locate one or more alternate writing spaces.

To Do

1. Make sure that you've secured a primary writing space, one where you do most of your writing, as discussed in Chapter 1.
2. Scout out a congenial alternate writing space. *dining room*
3. Add on additional spaces—a café, a park bench, a second room in your home. *Starbucks, park at Y*
4. Write everywhere.

CHAPTER 6

And Why Even Get Out of Bed?

Naturally you want a room in which to write that is dedicated to your writing pursuits and not the center of family commotion, the place where the canned goods are stored, or home to the water heater and the washer-dryer. But maybe you can't have such a dedicated room; maybe space is at a premium and all that's available to you is the kitchen table or a desk in your bedroom. Are you then hamstrung or limited? Not at all, not unless you consider yourself limited.

If you have a bed, you have an office. Writing is about thinking, feeling, and scribbling and can be done perfectly well while reclining. Colette, Proust, Walker Percy, Edith Wharton, James Joyce, my good friend whose novel just sold, our younger daughter who is working on her first novel, and countless other writers have written in bed and prefer to write there. What more do you need than your computer, your lap, your cup of coffee or tea, and warm feet?

Steve Denning explained, "Like many writers, I like writing in bed. I find this particularly relaxing with a laptop computer on a special table that fits over the bed. When you're lying in bed, you no longer have to worry about gravity. Your body is totally supported and your mind is free to float wherever its fancy leads it."

Maybe it's quite cold in the house. You could turn on the heat or you could save money and stay in bed with your writing. During the winter months of the war years 1941 through 1945, George Santayana did much of his writing in bed, wearing well-mended gloves in order to stay warm. The philosopher Irving Singer fluffs up his pillows, curls up in bed, and composes. "I do my best thinking when I am reclining," he explained. "Writing in bed defeats your inhibitions and allows the creative juices in your vegetative being to flow most freely."

The writing sisters Constance and Gwenyth Little, authors of a score of cult mystery classics, did all of their writing in bed. Tom and Enid Schantz explained, "If their screwball cozy mysteries were unusual, so was their writing regimen. They gleefully admitted to writing all of their books in bed. Constance thought of the plots, outlined them in great detail in large script, all from her bed, and then sent them over to Gwenyth, who did the rewrite and injected the humor, all from her bed."

The physical space you need is first of all the bubble in which you exist, your own atmosphere that extends a few inches in all directions beyond your skin and reaches as far as the keyboard of your computer. Next it is a corner of a room, a place where the rain doesn't fall and no one yells at you, fitted out with a chair and a table, or a sofa, or a stool, or an antique desk, or something else on the continuum from minimalist and functional to luxurious and functional. Next it is an enclosure, a room but also a room with a door, a place of privacy, a place meant for a working person to do his work. Beyond that it can be a library cubicle, a café table, a bench in a train station—any spot under the sun where a body might find himself or a body might set itself. But first of all it is the bubble in which you exist, in bed as well as anywhere else, defined by you, your pad, and your pen.

There is nowhere that you need to go in order to write, not even out of that bed. Right where you are is where your thoughts and feelings become available, if you are inclined to access them. Franz Kafka explained, "You do not need to leave your room. Remain sitting at your table and listen. The world will freely offer itself to you to be unmasked, it has no choice, it will roll in ecstasy at your feet." You can experience that ecstasy without even budging.

You don't have to deck out a fancy office in order to dream. Dreams come perfect and unbidden in bed, as you sit under an orange tree, as you stare out at the water, or when you sit quietly at your desk in front of drawn shades. They come to you on your sofa with jazz softly playing or in a busy café with life all around you.

First of all, they come to you while you sleep, dreams and good ideas both, fantasies and complete chapters. Isn't that proof that your primary physical space is between your ears, resting on a pillow, with the shades drawn or at most a sliver of moon for company?

LESSON 6

There is no place you need to go in order to write, not even out of bed. You are the writing machine, the writing space, everything.

To Do

1. Write a whole book in bed. See what that feels like.
2. Alternate writing spaces: a chapter in bed, a chapter at your desk, a chapter in bed, a chapter at your desk. See if that helps.
3. Invite someone into your bed. Collaborate—I mean on a writing project!
4. Organize your physical space so that it does the simple yet profound job of supporting your thinking, feeling, dreaming, and writing. Take out the distractions. Let everyone know the house rules. Supply yourself with all the necessary equipment and icons. If some itch remains, move the rubber ducky a little south or change the music—but at some point decide that your space isn't the issue, that your rubber ducky isn't a dybbuk, and that it is time to write. Just hop back into bed—but get writing.

Part II

Home Space

CHAPTER 7

Like Taking Your Medicine

Y ou're at home. But the faucet has a drip. The plants could be watered. The hall could be swept. You are at home, yes, where you do your writing, but writing isn't quite on the agenda right at this moment. You feel a little too muddle-headed to write; and then there's the drip, the parched ferns, and the dust bunnies. So, although you are at home, just a few feet from your writing, you might as well be in Kazakhstan, as close as you feel to writing.

So you wait. But waiting is very dangerous. If you wait for a time when your muddle-headedness, mild depression, to-do lists, doubts about the universe, and a thousand other things you could name are finally handled or settled, you will wait for a very long time. And as you wait, nothing good is happening; in fact, you are digging your hole deeper. No, waiting is a very dangerous game. Why don't you try the following instead?

Every four hours, just like taking your medicine, maybe at eight A.M., noon, four P.M., and eight P.M., ask yourself the following question: "Given the exact circumstances in which I find myself, am I able to write for fifteen minutes?" If your answer is no, explain to yourself why you are answering no. If your answer is yes but you don't start writing, explain to yourself why, even though you feel able to write, you aren't writing. If your answer is yes and you do write, have a chat with yourself about whether this writing stint would have occurred if you hadn't been checking in with yourself in this experimental way.

People who try this experiment typically report the following. "I wasn't able to write every four hours, as that seemed too artificial and arbitrary; and it also didn't work very well given the shape of my day. But I did notice that writing was much more on my mind and in fact I did turn to my writing more than I probably would have if I hadn't been thinking about those writing stints."

That's the point of this tactic: to keep your writing on your mind in such a front and center way that you're holding the intention to write even as you pull out the ironing board or pay your bills online. Whenever you find yourself at home, hold the intention to write, as that intention will translate into actual writing stints. However it is that you remember to take your medicine four times a day, do exactly the same with your writing.

Of course there's the risk that at your appointed time you'll find yourself unable to write; that by not writing you'll disappoint yourself; and as a consequence you'll feel even worse than if you hadn't tried at all. There is always the risk that you may disappoint yourself. That risk is there even for productive writers, as most writers don't write as often as they would like. Because of this reality, you will need to practice self-forgiveness. Just so long as you tie self-forgiveness to new resolve, it's smart not to badger yourself about any writing stints you skipped or any writing you failed to get accomplished.

We are very clever in the ways that we talk ourselves out of writing. Only rarely do we say, "I refuse to write today." More usually we say things like "I can't go shopping without a grocery list, so I had better get that list written" or "A little nap would be pleasant; no, more than pleasant, vital." By talking this way, we make sure that we don't notice that we're holding the strong intention to avoid our writing. The day goes by; some guilt accumulates; a little bitterness builds; maybe a little depression flowers. But on balance we've achieved our objectives: to avoid writing and to say nothing to ourselves that might alert us to our shenanigans.

By getting small, regular writing stints on the table, you get some writing-related inner talk going, even if it's of the "Oh, time to write—but I don't really feel up to it!" sort. That refusal, while disappointing, is nevertheless better than not thinking about your writing at all. You want to get a grip on your mind in such a way that your writing intentions exist in your thoughts. Planning your day around a series of writing stints helps with this.

Joan, a novelist, explained: "Continually holding the intention to write has caused my writing to feature more prominently in my life. Now I'm always mulling over the next paragraph, ruminating on it throughout the day, and thinking about where it's going to lead. Doing this regular 'intention holding' has given me a new freedom to think about the work, do the work, and allow the work to flow." You could wish to write, but that isn't quite strong enough. You could want to write, but that isn't strong enough either. Intend to write: that is the steelier orientation.

LESSON 7

Instead of scheduling one writing stint a day, schedule several. Wouldn't it be nice to write more than once a day?

To Do

1. Pick a day when you will be home all day.
2. Write four times that day, just as if you had medicine to take.
3. Write for those four stints; or for as many as you can.
4. Forgive yourself for any writing you didn't get done and commit to doing a better job of taking your medicine.

CHAPTER 8

The Space-Time Continuum

J have positive proof that the earth is slowing down and that soon we won't have gravity to contend with. My proof is the following. Every Wednesday morning Ann and I have the following conversation. Ann says, "The garbage goes out today." I say, "Right." Straightforward enough; except that Wednesday keeps arriving amazingly quickly. We just blink and there we are, saying those words again. "The garbage goes out today." "Right."

Since Wednesday has begun to arrive instantly, this must mean that time has speeded up, which means that the earth is slowing down. Elementary physics. You will remember from that physics text that cost you seventy-five dollars (and was worth it as a paperweight) that as you approach the speed of light, time slows down. If you could travel at the speed of light, you would never age. As to whether that would be a good thing or a bad thing, and how you could get a cup a coffee at 186,000 miles a second, I don't know. But that's the physics of the matter.

Since everyone's internal clock has sped up, the earth must be getting ready to stop its rotating. Even if that's bad physics—and I confess that it probably is—it's still good cultural reporting. Why do writers dream of spending a few months in Paris? Not for the Parisians, the weather, the Louvre, or even the baguettes (well, maybe for the baguettes). They dream of spending those months in Paris because they see themselves experiencing time differently there; they see themselves on café time. They see themselves not in a rush, neither externally nor internally. They see themselves actually stopping.

They see themselves quieted, finally, not through rough discipline or by dint of will but because the European café culture fully permits that stopping. Your waiter grants you that permission by not returning, not until you make some large gesture and boldly summon him. He respects the fact that you are slowing down time to a meditative crawl as you nurse your double espresso. He presumes that you have nothing to do more important than this—without presuming for an instant that you are an idler.

The waiter makes no such judgment. For all he knows (or cares) you worked for six straight hours earlier in the day, selling cars or fomenting a revolution, and will return to that work for another three hours after you leave his café. For now, though, time is appropriately stopped, making the fourth dimension an ally and not a thief. In our everyday life we steal our own neurons and we steal our time as well, rushing here, rushing there, committing one felony after another, until we have nothing left but those last fifteen minutes before bedtime—just enough time to feel disgusted by our own thievery.

When did we start rushing like this? Around 1880, I think, with the blooming of the Industrial Revolution and the introduction of the conveyor belt. I think the conveyor belt is the culprit, coupled with that famous Lucy episode. Or maybe it began with *Sesame Street* and its style of fast cutting, which created culture-wide ADHD. Or maybe it's a more contemporary phenomenon connected to video games and the global ideal of business at the speed of light. Whatever its precise date of birth, it's been a hundred years in the making and now we've perfected it: perfected the rat race, complete with text messaging.

Today, even when we're sitting still we're speeding. We're anticipating our next cell phone call, awaiting our next e-mail, entering or leaving some chat room, and running a race that can't be won. The finish line is moving right along with us, keeping perfect pace because the gods want us to feel ridiculous. I presume that you picture the same gods that I do, ironic ones who love to watch us meditate and then rush out the door to accomplish sixty-eight thousand things before dinner. Can't you see them pointing and laughing: "As if twenty minutes of meditating is going to stop her inner rat race!"

When time has taken this nasty turn and begun speeding up, such that a walk on the beach becomes a jog and a weeklong retreat in our rented Maine cabin becomes 618,000 seconds of racing monkey mind, we are obliged to acknowledge that we are out of control. We are like the passengers on that bus in *Speed*, the bus remote-controlled by a fiend, and we are terrified, exactly as they were, that if we slow down we will explode. What a place we have landed, to fear thirty minutes of silence.

If, because the week has sped by, it is always Wednesday, and you are always getting ready to take out the garbage, what does it matter if you have the perfect writing space? You are like Alice falling down the rabbit hole, able to grab a pill or a bite to eat but in no way able to write *Wuthering Heights*. Time is racing; you are falling; and just imagine—there is nothing necessary about any of this. This is nothing but an experience you are permitting. You could right your time ship by simply penciling in two hours and announcing, "I will experience this time as slow, quiet, precious, and full of my writing." You could right your time ship just like that.

There is objective time of the sort kept at the Greenwich Observatory, muddled in Indiana (where neighboring towns find themselves in different time zones) and marching along no matter how we rail at it. Then there is our experience of time, which is a psychological, social, and cultural matter. We do not experience time the same way when we are depressed as when we are manic, when we are trapped in a duck blind as when we are crouched there of our own volition, or when we are typing away on our opus as when we are wringing our hands over a comma. As much as we want more time, even more than that we need to monitor our experience of time. That's the challenge.

When you carefully monitor your experience of time, then you don't mind if time races by, not if you are immersed and engrossed and, after three hours, look down to discover seven pages of your novel completed. That is good speed. What you don't want is your life to speed by in the pursuit of nothing. Speed is not the issue; time is not the issue; the issue is the quality of your life. When you find yourself at home in your writing space, hush your mind, hold your dream, open to your work, and time will take care of itself. It may pass in slow motion, it may race by, or it may stop altogether: none of that is an issue, not if you are lost in the writing.

LESSON 8

There is time per se. Then there is time as experience. You want to carve out hours for your writing and you want to experience those hours in a certain way, your mind undistracted, your heart open, your watch broken.

To Do

1. Slow down time by watching the second hand of an old-fashioned clock for five full minutes. Experience the fantastic length and abundance of those five minutes. Isn't it enough time to create a whole world, right down to the lampposts and the street signs?
2. Stop racing around as if someone had lodged a jet engine in your shorts.
3. Replicate café time at your own desk, from 5:00 A.M. to 7:00 A.M. each morning, as you quietly create your masterpiece.
4. Take the time or waste the time. Your choice.

CHAPTER 9

At Home, Choosing

Every day, writers must make choices: about which piece of writing to tackle, about whether to write for twenty minutes or for three hours, about whether to abandon a difficult piece or revise it one more time, about whether to put the comma in or take the comma out. They must also make choices, at least as hard as their writing choices, about whether, how, and to what extent to market their work. Is this the day to update the Web site, propose a column, schedule some talking engagements, or engage in some networking?

If you are already choosing to write and choosing to market in a regular way, you may not need to institute the following practice. But all of us can benefit from this mindful way of living the writing life. Every day, say, "I choose to write today. This means that I will _____" and fill in the blank appropriately. For instance:

I choose to write today. This means that I will

- return to Chapter 3 of my novel for at least an hour
- commit to beginning my memoir even though I'm afraid of offending my parents
- start that article that feels a little bit boring but that would probably be wanted in the marketplace
- walk the beach and let my swirling ideas settle, then write for an hour at the rib joint by the beach (then have ribs!)
- go directly to my writing
- deal with the unwieldy transition between Chapter 2 and Chapter 3
- decide whether to write John out of the novel or figure out how to make him much more lively

Occasionally, at least once a week and maybe even daily, especially if you are hoping to build your platform or have several projects to market, say, "I choose to market today. This means that I will _____" and fill in the blank appropriately. For instance:

I choose to market today. This means that I will

- try to get some early endorsements for my nonfiction book idea

- make a list of twelve literary agents to query about my novel
- tackle writing the synopsis of my novel
- find an Internet site to query about my column idea
- invite my contacts to subscribe to my newsletter (and then write my first newsletter!)
- find some way to give a talk about my subject, so that I can get comfortable with public speaking
- visit the sites of the five small presses that might be interested in my poetry collection

For the coming week, try out both sets of sentences ("I choose to write today. This means that I will" and "I choose to market today. This means that I will") on a daily basis.

Mark, a novelist, gave this a try. He reported: "This choosing to write daily and then defining the action I'm going to take is powerful. It sets the intention right off and then creates a kind of mini-plan. I've been doing it all week and the writing's been getting done this way without a lot of struggle getting to the computer. What gets worked on and for how long becomes the 'conversation,' not whether to write or how to find the time to write."

Joanne, a nonfiction writer, explained: "The word 'today' is a very useful one for me. Although I did not ask myself these questions every day, I did ask one or the other of them on most days; and having the time limitation of 'today' embedded in each was very useful. In the past, I have tended to get overwhelmed, feeling that everything must be done in some amorphous 'now.' Asking one specific working question at a time, focusing on one writing priority for one creative day at a time, has been a useful device.

"I've also noticed that it's important for me to get a balance between writing and marketing. When I focused primarily on marketing for a few days, I became crabby in that way that happens when I am away from a daily connection to my writing. In the midst of this frustrating stretch of marketing efforts, I found that I had to return to my writing. But when I don't ask myself what am I going to do to market my work, I also get frustrated. So the next step is to use these focusing sentences and become aware of the patterns of work that balance me as a productive writer and a productive saleswoman."

Max, a screenwriter, explained: "One day this week I decided that I would only have time to read over a part of my screenplay and, because I had been so specific in my planning, I did manage to make the time to do it, even though I felt really tired. This way of choosing what to write each day feels just right: it helps me feel calm and very clear in my own mind about the writing projects I want to tackle.

"Yesterday, for instance, because my writing choices were written out, late in the day I happened upon my list and realized that I'd forgotten my intentions. So I squeezed a little writing in.

But I'd like to do better than this and not just 'happen on my list.' I recognize that I don't have this habit in place yet and I just have to keep working at it."

Each day that you find yourself at home, even for just the few hours before work and the few hours after work, choose to get some writing done and some marketing done. To do that, you may have to crack through your resistance, fight through your fatigue, and have a chat with yourself about why writing is the better choice than flipping on the television. You may have to splash cold water on your face, quiet your fears about entering the mysterious space of your new novel, and skip certain "pressing" duties, such as analyzing the day's junk mail. None of that may come easily. But you have that choice.

Home is a funny place. It is the place to unwind, watch a movie, kick off your shoes, and drop your public persona. It is the place to read a magazine, surf the Internet, and return a few phone calls. But if you are a writer, it is also your office. It is your place of business. It is the place where you think hard as well as relax. It is the place where you suffer some as you try to get your writing ideas worked out, so it is not always a cheerful place. It can't always be a happy, kick-off-your-shoes kind of place: if it is, you aren't writing and you aren't selling.

This means that you have to enter into a complex relationship with your home space, one defined by a critical daily choice: how much of the time you will be "at home" and how much of the time you will be "at work." Maybe you can make some clear distinctions, for instance that when you are in your study you are "working" and when you leave it you are "at home" again. But such neatness is hard to maintain. What if an idea comes to you unbidden when you are doing the dishes? Will you tell it to come back later, when you're back in your study? No; you'll be forced to make the kind of choice we've been discussing throughout: to be a writer, or not to be.

LESSON 9

The writing life is defined by the succession of choices you make, primary among them whether or not you will write.

To Do

1. Answer the following question: "How can I construct my home life around the fact that home is where I both relax and work?"
2. Every day, make a concrete (though simple) plan for your writing life—for instance, "Today I will write from six A.M. to eight A.M."
3. At least several days a week, make a concrete (though simple) plan for your marketing life—for instance, "Today I'll write two sample columns."
4. Choose writing.

CHAPTER 10

Your Mind on Brownies

In the pieces to come we'll chat about the dark and the light: the dark of emotional disturbance, stolen neurons, and meaning crises, the light of worlds birthed, park-bench musings, and you sitting at your desk with a smile and a bright idea.

A writer's space is just like that, dark and light, and more gossamer and golden the more you can manage your moods, write to your satisfaction, and enjoy some successes. As a sensible creature, you certainly don't expect round-the-clock sunshine. But you do expect some excellent pleasures. Here are some of them.

It is quiet. You have a lovely idea for a book. You take your laptop out to the living room sofa. No one is around. You boot up your laptop. Your idea is percolating; you can feel some richness coming. You make yourself a cup of white pomegranate tea and pull out the pan of brownies from the refrigerator.

Should you cut yourself a small piece, a medium-sized piece, or a large piece? This is such a lucky hour that you go for the large. You are ready: big brownie, hot tea, and the fine pressure of delivery. The light is subdued but ample; the world is hushed; you open a new file and see a blank page appear. Even the morning stars stop twinkling so as not to distract you.

You begin. Nothing is in the way. Your physical space is a joy. Your emotional space is clear. Your neurons are firing. Your fingers move and a sentence appears. It is beautiful from beginning to end, pregnant with meaning, exactly what you intended, and as good a start to this journey as you could have asked for. It is so fine a start that the next sentence tumbles right out, dying to join the first.

This is a good hour. No sugar blues, only sugar happiness. No doubts, only enthusiasm. No minced ideas, only serendipity. You continue. Whole pages come. On some days 500 words exhaust you; today you find yourself on page nine so suddenly that you wonder if you're in a parallel universe, one where writing is easy.

You have no need to reread what you've written; you know that it's working. Another thousand words come and that's that, that's all your brain can manage. But you've put almost four thousand words down on paper, a twentieth of your book, good words, words as good as words get. You created a world that when you awoke didn't exist; and you just know that other human beings like yourself will be happy to experience this world, that your imagined world will become their vicarious home for the few hours they visit it.

You never did finish your brownie. You remember taking a few bites and then you vanished into the writing. Now you heat up your half-cup of tea and luxuriate with it and the excellent remaining brownie chunk. It is very smooth but also very nutty, the perfect brownie, not unlike this perfect writing day.

As soon as you finish your tea and brownie a wisp of a meaning crisis drifts by: you've written, you've had your brownie, and now what? But you smile, shake your head, and decide where you will make your next meaningful investment. You will do a little writing business. You are just in the mood for feeling like a real writing professional, someone who segues effortlessly from making magic to selling product.

You sit back and dream a whole series into existence, one that starts with the book you began to birth this morning and that takes readers on a splendid journey through many volumes. You create the series in an hour and spend another few hours polishing your vision and making sure of your intentions. Then you craft the sales piece describing the series, the rhetorically powerful sales piece that will cause editors to drool and pull out their checkbooks.

But wait! The day isn't over yet. While you were dreaming your series into existence you were, unbeknownst to yourself, also still working on your book. Now another few thousand words of that book demand to be gathered. You gather them; it becomes evening; you have hardly moved from your spot all day long. Now for some dinner! Could a writer have a better day?

Fortunately this doesn't happen every day or we would be insufferably happy. But we are glad that it happens occasionally. No, the writing life is more than tumbleweed and sandpaper, addictions and mental lapses, chill winds and botched endings. Some days, it is the best thing on earth. Some days, it is the kind of thing that makes even a sad mortal quietly smile. Some days, it is amazing.

And what if we never experience a perfect writing day? We write anyway. We write anyway, because we are the sort of creature who sees something at the age of seven, and something else when we are fifteen, and knows that it is our destiny—one of our destinies—to pull that all together into a fine piece of fiction that would also make an excellent movie. It is only one of our destinies, as we can also go in that other direction, in the direction of not writing. But who wants to go there?

LESSON 10

It is your destiny to write, but it is only a potential destiny. Assure your fate by creating right space and living and working there.

To Do

1. Make absolutely sure that you have a primary writing space. Then write there, serious in your meaning intentions.
2. Go there now.
3. Bring along a brownie and a cup of tea.
4. Have a splendid writing day. And if it isn't splendid, write anyway.

Part III

Mind Space

CHAPTER 11

Your New Impeccability

Writing is what you do when you compose an e-mail. Creating is what you do when you compose *War and Peace*. To paraphrase Mark Twain, the first resembles the second as the lightning bug resembles lightning. The movement from composing an e-mail to composing War and Peace isn't quantitative: it isn't the process of stringing ten thousand e-mails together. It isn't the process of writing 250 words every day or writing for an hour every day. Rather, it is the act of stepping off a cliff and tumbling, in total bewilderment, head-over-heels through creative space.

The writer looking to do some interesting work on her novel, screenplay, essay, or poem is obliged to remember that her mind is not as easy to use as a can opener and that her personality is not as easy to remove as an overcoat. She likely needs to move—

not from Boise to New York, not from her Jungian therapist to a Freudian therapist, not from workshop to workshop, but from her current way of being to a different space, to "right inner space." What does right inner space look like? How do you get there and stay there? Those are our questions.

The first thing you have to do in order to acquire right inner space is to shed your everyday personality. You have to stop being somebody's daughter, somebody's wife, somebody who worries about the weather and the price of apples, somebody who got humiliated in third grade by Mrs. Lester, somebody who hasn't written enough these past twenty years, somebody who furiously cleans if company is coming, somebody who . . . you need to shed all of that! You need to shed all of that and become a weightless, boundless mind whose body and wardrobe are just along for the ride.

Unfortunately, you can't slip out of your personality like a snake discards its skin. Your personality is inside every cell and molecule of your being. Therefore you must disintegrate, evaporate, and vanish, in order to reintegrate, condense, and reappear as a creative writer. Right inner space arrives only after your own magnificent demolition and reconstruction. That's why you may not have been writing enough. That's why it may have taken you three years to write a draft of your novel that still isn't really done or really adequate. You never stopped to blow yourself up.

You never stopped being the person bogged down in mind chatter and shackled to the firing of worried thoughts. Picture one of those Las Vegas hotels getting demolished. That's what needed to happen!

How are you supposed to accomplish this magnificent demolition and reconstruction? Wait: we had better address the dangers first. The primary danger in agreeing to create, rather than in agreeing to merely write, is that you are agreeing to throw over your everyday being and turn yourself into a vehicle run by your imagination. You are agreeing to stand perplexed for a whole year as your plot works itself out, agitated for every second of that year as this idea and then that idea spills out from your firing neurons, all those tumbling ideas demanding to be understood, evaluated, accepted, or rejected.

You are agreeing to a new impeccability, where every word, every paragraph, and every idea you set down on paper has to pass muster, not in the first draft but eventually. You are agreeing to bleed for your art on days when your ideas torture you. Do not nod and agree to risk your equanimity and to live tumultuously unless you mean it. Maybe you didn't quite understand what was being asked of you when, previously, you casually agreed that you were willing to take some risks for the sake of your writing. I hope that the matter is clearer to you now. If it is, it is time to get a new agreement in place.

Now you are really agreeing to unleash your creativity. You are agreeing to turn over your inner life to your art. You are agreeing to create right inner space in which worlds and not mere sentences are born. In that space great and horrible collisions will occur. You accept that, embrace that, and refuse to flinch from that. In that space worlds regularly explode. Get ready! If you agree, scribble across this page: "I agree!" (Unless this is a library book.)

It is good to have this agreement in place. I hope that you're excited. You just agreed to be a creative machine, a creative whirlwind, a creative daredevil. Congratulations! Now we can begin.

The first step in creating right inner space is that you vanish. You manage your personality, your neuroses, your dramas, your foments, your excuses, your doubts, your regrets, your parents' admonitions, the constricting feel of your first-grade classrooms and become no one, everyone, and a god or a goddess. You become your potential! You actually become your potential.

You do this shedding in the following way: by recovering those billions of neurons that are presently trapped thinking thoughts of no particular use to you. You become a truly creative person by recovering your mind. More on that in a moment.

LESSON 11

To be a writer you must write, but being a writer is not about writing. The next time you worry your brain about whether you can write, slap yourself hard. Everyone can write. Your worry should be whether you are brave enough to vanish into the depths of your neuronal circuitry and come back with creations. You are a diver, not a writer; an explorer, not a writer; an inventor, not a writer; a magician, not a writer.

To Do

1. Agree to be creative. Don't agree if you don't mean it.
2. Agree to give up every excuse you have ever employed to avoid getting your writing done. You know what they are: that you are too busy, too tired, too far behind, too burdened by that mean-spirited spouse, too tall to sit comfortably at your desk, too unhappy, too computer illiterate, too constrained by responsibilities, too cold in the morning, too. . . .
3. Stop being the you that doesn't serve you.
4. Open up to a great piece of fiction-shaped or nonfiction-shaped imagining. Begin it!

CHAPTER 12

Self-Help for Neurons

H ow can you release your billions of neurons from their slavish grip on remembering your brother-in-law's telephone number and your favorite color? Well, first the idea has to make sense to you. You have to agree with my contention that knowing the birthdates of everyone in your family, down to Cousin Marvin and Aunt Rose, costs you whole books and whole decades of your writing life.

You have to recognize the following: that minding a worry as if you are minding an infant, such that the worry is never far from consciousness and losing sight of it for an instant causes you to start scurrying around the apartment searching for it, is not some innocent neurotic handicap but a complete self-theft program. It is the perfect way to steal billions of neurons from your meager many billions, leaving you stupider and less imaginative. How clever is that?

It is time to stop giving away billions of your neurons to task maintenance, memory maintenance, and worry maintenance. Isn't it?

It is one thing to have a worry when it is appropriate to have a worry. The day before your Nobel Prize acceptance speech, it is appropriate to put in for a wake-up call and to worry that your request hasn't quite registered in the eyes of the handsome Swedish desk clerk. Given your worry, you say, "Did you get that? I need to get up tomorrow. The king is expecting me." Experience teaches us whether or not the quality of the clerk's response reassures us or continues to worry us. If it continues to worry us, we sidle down the counter to another clerk, smile, and exclaim, "I need a wake-up call tomorrow at five A.M.! Can you help me?" We continue smiling when she pushes a few buttons and curtly replies, "Sir, that has been taken care of!"

Then we forget about it.

If we've been worried about that wake-up call for the three months leading up to Stockholm, we probably haven't written our acceptance speech yet, and shame on us! On the other hand, if we know perfectly well that there are plenty of things to worry about, from today's gulag to the escalating price of tangerines, but refuse to turn over a single neuron to mere unproductive worry, then we'll have sufficient neurons available to write a really excellent acceptance speech, like the one Aleksandr Solzhenitsyn wrote, so fine a speech that it is available in paperback.

A famous Zen parable, slightly mangled in the retelling, goes as follows. Master and disciple are out walking. They come to a deep, fast-rushing stream and encounter a damsel in distress who, perhaps because she prefers not to get her skirt wet, is stuck on this side of the stream. She asks the master to carry her across. Because of the ascetic tradition that they practice, the disciple presumes that the master will say no.

Lo and behold, the master agrees and carries her across. Master and disciple proceed on their merry way, the disciple brooding about (or envious of) the fact that his teacher got to touch a lady. Back at the monastery, the disciple confronts the master, exclaiming, "How could you do that? We are expressly forbidden to touch a woman!" The master smiles benignly (or else whacks him with a stick—I forget) and replies, "Are you still thinking about that woman? I left her at the riverbank and look, you are still carrying her around!"

The master can get on with his next haiku. His student, by contrast, seems doomed—until he is enlightened, or just a little smarter—to turn over billions of his neurons to brooding about his master's conduct and parsing the distinction between an injunction against touching and the offer of a helping hand. Probably another few billion neurons will get devoted to fantasizing about that woman. The disciple is unable to empty his mind, a task that is the exact equivalent of returning neurons to the fold.

A free neuron, unencumbered by the demand to do a bit of work—to connect with his buddies in the service of remembering how many husbands a certain celebrity has cycled through or to link in a sad daisy chain of remembrance about the time we didn't get that red bicycle—is an available neuron, quiet as a church mouse: hence the experience of profound silence that comes with "quiet mind." Get all your neurons back and, voilà! you have silence, presence, and the sort of mind space that attracts leaps of imagination.

Too many stolen neurons and you aren't actually present. Oh, sure, you look like a writer, sitting there in front of your computer, chewing on your nail and playing with a swell Italian word whose lilt charms you. But it is only your body and a too-small percentage of your brain that you've brought to the task. It is like coming to a singing contest with half a vocal cord or to an eating contest with your stomach stapled. You look fine to the judges, who may even peg you for a favorite, but you don't stand a chance.

The essence of presence is freeing neurons. You say that you are intending to write, and certainly part of you means that. But a billion neurons are gripping the weather forecast. Another billion are holding your upset about eating (or not eating) breakfast. Another billion—no, several!—are infamously linked to remind you that the first sentence you write today will prove that you are an idiot and an imposter. Virtually every neuron you own is already charged with some task and the remaining few can't help but whimper, "You want us to dream up a great novel?"

It is hard to say where you are, neuronally speaking, when you deliver over billions of your neurons to unnecessary facts, sneaky feelings, and mounds of fluff and nonsense. But it's not ready to write. Of course, you can still write, just as the world's work force can send e-mails all day long even though trillions of their neurons are elsewhere. But that is not our kind of writing. That is not the writing you fell down on your knees in front of when you happened upon a good book. To do our writing, you need those neurons back. You may have sent them away, but now you must recall them in all seriousness.

LESSON 12

There is some delicate, delectable material up there in your head, neurons and synapses and neural transmitters and all sorts of fancy machinery that the universe has gone to a lot of trouble to create for writers. Don't waste it by turning neurons over to tasks that are the equivalent of getting your socks matched. Every freed neuron is a tiny fraction of a great idea and you—and only you—are its liberator.

To Do

1. Forget your brother-in-law's phone number. You've got it stored in your electronic address book, don't you? Get back 163,000,000 neurons right there.

2. Practice letting thoughts not only come but go. Think "Weeds in the garden" and let the thought, the sting, the command, the demand, the big drama around weeds just evaporate. Don't give a billion of your stray neurons even a nanosecond to join hands and create the mischief of a guilt trip.

3. Remember your wife's birthday but forget your own. Do you really care when you were born? Isn't it more important to care about being alive? Make strict choices about where you will employ neurons. When something comes up, ask yourself "Is that worth three billion neurons?"

4. Get a grip on your mind, which means helping neurons surrender their iron grip. Isn't that a charming paradox?

Chapter 13

Pluto's Not a Planet Anymore

When Pluto got demoted, I spontaneously composed and began singing a song called "Pluto's Not a Planet Anymore," rhyming "astronomer" with "barometer" and, for the two hours it took us to drive from San Francisco to the Gold Country, making our visiting daughters crazy.

"Stop!" they cried. But I found it impossible to stop, their poking notwithstanding, because Pluto's demotion struck a deep chord within me. It wasn't the chord that it struck almost universally, in every town and city in America. Most people were annoyed, dismayed, and even heartbroken that a sure fact of existence, that our solar system comprised nine planets, had turned out be an unsure thing after all. That, however, was not my reaction.

I was not annoyed, dismayed, or heartbroken. I was amused, amused that suddenly everyone had to share, ready or not, in the writer's constant fate, that solid things turn liquid on a daily basis. For the irreverent and painful morphing of things is as integral to the process of writing as adding sugar is to the making of Christmas cookies. If, as a writer, you want your planets to stay put, are you ever in for some disturbing surprises and rude awakenings!

People want exactly that: solid ground. When they come in to work they want their desk to be where they left it, they want the operating system on their computer to be unchanged, they want the person in the next cubicle to be the same person they said goodbye to yesterday at closing time. If all of this were to change from one day to the next they would feel disoriented at best, crazy at worst, and in desperate need of a drink, a drug, or an explanation.

If you are a writer, forget about solid ground. Here is what happens to you. You start a suspense novel about a Navy wife who learns something she shouldn't know. Three days in, you find your plot uninteresting. Oh, it's interesting enough, just not to you. You can imagine somebody else writing your novel and even enjoying writing it, but to you it is just work. Why spend two years on the intricacies of double agents and triple agents when you couldn't care less?

So you change it. You make it a novel about four Navy wives and recast it as an atmospheric drama about betrayal and loss. But after a week of writing you discover that only two of the wives actually interest you. The other two are there simply because you think you need four wives, because you read somewhere that "four women" novels are invariably successful. You sleep poorly and wish that someone would kidnap two of your wives—maybe someone from Book 1.

Book 2 stalls. Should it be about the two wives you like? If so, what is it now actually about? Where's the suspense? Where's the juice? What's the point? You could get them together and make it a Navy Lesbian Wife novel and maybe start a new genre, but that really wasn't your intention and besides you would have to do all that research. . . .

In the middle of the night it comes to you that if you set it two hours north of Berlin in a small German town you once visited where they drink that cheap grog whose name you can't remember and where you got really drunk and recast it as a novel about two German women who teach at a small art college . . . but where in God's name did THAT come from?

Our author of this morphing novel needs a name. Let's call her Cassandra. The universe's tricksters already plague Cassandra. Her hair is never quite the right length or color, pounds creep on while she is sleeping, the man in her life refuses to work, either because he is inept, passive-aggressive, or too much in love with hockey, and her father, whom she would love to hate, had the gall to die, and how easy is it to hate a dead man? Now her novel is doing this constant morphing thing. It is really too much; and even throwing darts at an effigy of Hemingway doesn't help. It is as if the television set of her mind were controlled by Rod Serling and, in her particular Twilight Zone, she had to watch two minutes of bass fishing followed by thirty seconds of that infomercial about buying resort property in Texas. . . .

What is Cassandra to do? Hang in there. Allow her brain to take her from a Navy base in Maryland to a small town in northern Germany to wherever it will take her next, hoping against hope that when it lands on solid ground and the novel she actually means to write arises she will know it; and that the ground will remain solid for eighteen months straight as she writes that darned (always threatening to morph again) novel. She must hang in there exactly as a trapeze artist hangs in there, tumbling through thin air and trusting that her partner's hands will appear out of nowhere to grab her wrists.

You must hang in there, even though the "there" is thin air.

In my own case, I am trying to follow up a recent novel with a sequel in which the main character from the first novel, a feisty New York painter, finds herself at risk in the heartland. Of only one thing am I certain: that there will be a midnight raft trip down the Ohio, a homage to Huck Finn, a flight under a full moon from Full Moon, Indiana. But I hope that the word "certain" in that sentence made you fall out of your chair laughing. Who can say whether that midnight raft ride down the Ohio won't turn into a subway ride through Barcelona by tomorrow evening? Only my dancing neurons can say—and they are busy dancing.

Yes, all this morphing can prove our downfall. By contrast, Pluto's demotion is purely cosmetic. It had a downfall by definition only; it is the still same happy, arid, freezing spheroid it was yesterday and a billion years ago. Cassandra's novel, by contrast, is nothing like it was when it was a thriller about double agents or a "four women" novel. Right now, it is just potential energy, weird ideas, and shifting landscapes. I tell you, Pluto has it easy.

Maybe Neptune will get the ax next. Neither Cassandra nor I will care much. We have books to trap in our consciousness that, like greased pigs, are running and squealing and morphing, not into nice slabs of bacon but into animals undreamed of by gods or by Darwin. All that squealing is addling and the grease is hard to get off your synapses. But there are no alternatives. Maybe you could buy some software that would do the thinking for you— but does that sound promising?

Hang in there, in thin air. It is precarious; but my what a view!

LESSON 13

In the space between your ears, more morphing will occur than has happened in the whole history of natural selection. That makes you something of a god, but a powerless, wacky, and demented one. Enjoy your divinity. If you would like it to be otherwise, better drive a cab or run a corporation. In our mad world, where books appear, we must live with the spectacular nature of the creative process, where profusion and confusion dance together.

To Do

1. Change your name to Cassandra. Why not?
2. Tell yourself "Each book is an adventure." Mean it, as it is the truth.
3. Do not feel bad for Pluto. It only has to go round and round. You have to ride the wind in a tornado, grabbing scenes as they fly by along with the uprooted trees, the Dorothies, and the Totos.
4. Expect change. Wild change. The kind of change that sends nine out of ten writers packing—but not you.

CHAPTER 14

Creative Mindfulness

J'm sure you agree with me that your mind is your gold and that you do not want the vagaries of circumstance and personality to rob you of your rich imaginings. How exactly do you prevent that theft and recover that pregnant silence in which your freed neurons can connect the universe's dots? You prevent that theft by the practice of creative mindfulness, which is a step up from ordinary mindfulness.

The word "mindfulness" has a long definitional tradition and a particular meaning. It stands for the nonjudgmental observation and acknowledgment of our thoughts. We notice the thought— for example, "I am running from my writing"—and acknowledge that we had that thought. It comes, we notice it, it goes. The central goal of ordinary mindfulness is to let such a thought come and go without experiencing pain, without holding on to it, without turning it into a monster that eats us alive.

Traditional mindfulness is an excellent practice. Current studies prove conclusively that a mindfulness meditation practice improves your health and your sense of well-being. If you school yourself in just this limited practice, you will have done wonders for your equanimity. But you will not yet be fully awake, fully functioning, or ready to create. You will have taken a first enormous step: you will have arrived at a place of fearlessly looking at and accepting the contents of your thoughts. But more is needed.

It is excellent to know that you are thinking "I am running from my writing." It is excellent to be able to experience that thought without sinking into pain and despair. But observing that thought without pain or judgment is not the same thing as resuming your writing. The goal of a creativity mindfulness practice is not the nonjudgmental observation of our thoughts but complete right thinking that leads to reams of writing and oodles of mental health. Our goal is not to be calm, centered, or even enlightened, but to be all of that and also to write like a wild person.

The central goal of traditional mindfulness is that when you eat a potato, you really eat that potato. The goal of creative mindfulness is that when you eat that potato, you really eat that potato and you also work on your novel. Being present for that potato is not your highest goal; that is too simple, mechanical, and even immoral an understanding of the point of presence. It makes it seem as if being present for that potato is more important than mindfully planning, as you eat your French fry, how to free political prisoners, end a war, or plot your screenplay. It overrates the simple act of noticing and can easily lead to disengagement and inaction.

Jon Kabat-Zinn explained, "Mindfulness means paying attention in a particular way: on purpose, in the present moment, and nonjudgmentally. This kind of attention nurtures greater awareness, clarity, and acceptance of present-moment reality."

Thich Nhat Hanh echoed this idea: "While washing the dishes one should only be washing the dishes, which means one should be completely aware of the fact that one is washing the dishes. I am completely myself, following my breath, conscious of my presence, and conscious of my thoughts and actions."

The high ideal of "creative mindfulness" is to master mindfulness, in the sense in which Jon Kabat-Zinn, Thich Nhat Hanh, and others have described it, and to employ that mastery in the service of deep thought, rich action, and wide-awake living of the sort Thoreau envisioned when he wrote "Millions of people are awake enough for physical labor; but only one in a million is awake enough for effective intellectual exertion, only one in a hundred million to a poetic or divine life. We must learn to reawaken and keep ourselves awake."

Here are the six principles of creative mindfulness:

1. *Fearlessly observe your own thoughts.* All of your excuses, all the ways you unhinge yourself, all of your dodges, all of your secret complaints and sources of pain, are right there in the thoughts you are thinking. Awaken to knowledge of your own thoughts.

2. *Detach from the thoughts you are thinking.* This means that you confidently observe each thought with a certain curiosity, sanguine assurance, and phlegmatic and philosophic distance, such that you comprehend it but are not smacked around by it. What you are really detaching from is the pain, sting, or charge attached to your thoughts. Then you can tolerate a thought like "I am fleeing from my writing" long enough to deal with it productively.

3. *Appraise your thoughts.* You are not judgmental but you are a wise judge. When you hear yourself think "I am fleeing from my writing," you do not excoriate yourself; rather, you stop to appraise the truth or falsity of that thought, make sense of its implications, and decide what you want to do in light of your appraisal. That is, you stop and think.

4. *Restate your intentions based on your appraisal.* If, after thinking about it, you decide that you do not want to run from your novel, think the new thought that aligns with that positive intention—for instance, "I think I'll stop running

now." Respond to the appraised thought with your new understanding and your new commitment.

5. *Free your neurons, empty your mind, and ready yourself for creating.* Ordinary mindfulness is the observation of thought. Creative mindfulness requires that you vanish, your mind hushed, so that your creative thoughts can appear. Observe, appraise, and restate, then open to an ever-deepening silence.

6. *Explode into your work.*

To summarize: observe, detach, appraise, restate, empty, and explode. This might sound like: "Oh, I am fleeing from my novel. How horrible! What a weakling I am! I feel so much pain thinking that! But wait. Let me just be with that thought. 'I am fleeing from my novel.' All right. Let me say it again without judging me in the process: 'I am fleeing from my novel.' Okay. I think I can tolerate hearing that. Whew. That is one very hard thought to think. Damn! Okay, easy. 'I am fleeing from my novel.' Okay. That's the truth of the matter. I am honestly appraising the situation and I must conclude that I have had a true thought. Okay. Easy. That is a bitter pill to swallow but I am okay. What do I want to do? I want to resume that novel. Yes, I do. I really do! So I am going to think the following thought: 'I've been fleeing from my novel but I won't run from it any longer.' Okay. Let me take that in. Okay. Now all I need to do is get quiet, free my neurons, empty my head, and let my novel return with a big whoosh!"

This sounds much noisier and busier on the page than it will sound in your own brain. In your own brain, you can move from complaint, doubt, distraction, and self-treason to complete freedom and immersion in a nanosecond, by following the principles of creative mindfulness. You can do it in the blink of an eye, just by adopting the right orientation and holding the right intention.

The day will come when fewer painful thoughts plague you because you have turned your life around through the practice of creative mindfulness. But there will never come a time when your thinking won't produce some amount of pain, difficulty, anxiety, doubt, and despair. You will need to constantly attend to your creative mindfulness practice: that is the only way to keep your "mind space" healthy and productive.

LESSON 14

Mind space is your main space. You can fill it up with clutter and chatter, you can let its contents sink you into depression, or you can aim for creative mindfulness and mind mastery. You are a slave to every thought of which you are not the master.

To Do

1. Learn to observe your thoughts, detach from your thoughts, appraise your thoughts, restate your intentions, empty your mind, and explode into your art.
2. Really learn this.
3. Really, really learn this.
4. Produce a thought you hate, such as "I haven't written in a month," and practice creative mindfulness.

Part IV

Emotional Space

CHAPTER 15

Emotional Intelligence for Writers

Y ou get angry. You get envious. You get depressed. You are not a stone. Nor do you want to be a stone. You have no intention of not feeling. You have no intention of taming your emotions so well that you end up domesticated and limp. You want your full measure of emotion, as emotion is the lifeblood of art. Emotion is the surest sign that you are alive, the deepest motivator, and the edge that causes your knife to cut. Of course you intend to live with emotion.

But that doesn't mean that you should be a slave to your emotions. Say that you hear about a writer getting a big advance. Do you want to feel bad for a week or do you want to let the pain go in a split second? Say that an editor criticizes your short story. Do you want to writhe in agony or do you want to laugh at the blowoff? Say that you've had nothing published for two years.

Do you want to sink into despair and end up drinking turpentine or do you want to demand of yourself continued optimism and shout out that you are not dead and not defeated?

In each case, you should want the latter from yourself. There is no good point in allowing your feelings to rule you as if you were a rag doll puppet. If you let your emotions rule you, you will use your newly sharpened pencil not to write the excellent novel waiting to be written but to stab yourself in the heart. You want to master your emotions, not be their slave. If you think that is too tall an order, think again. Remember the time that you decided that you didn't want to feel a certain way any longer, shook the feeling off, and felt better instantly? See, you can do it!

All the emotions that sometimes get you down—the pain, discouragement, bitterness, self-disgust, rage, sorrow, emptiness, hollowness, envy, fear—may well rear up automatically and reflexively in response to a stimulus. But in the next split second, the emotion having arrived, you get to decide whether you will embrace it and invite it to stay or whether you will meet it with mindful resolve and show it the door. You can quickly and efficiently deal with an unwanted emotion the split second after it arrives: that is what emotional mastery means.

Mindfulness includes minding your emotions. If you know that it will rile you to reread that curt e-mail from that literary agent, delete it. What are you saving it for? Are you saving it just to rile yourself up, or for the day when exactly the right retort will come to your mind and you can get even, or to forward it to your friend the hit man who owes you a favor? Delete it. Let it go. That is the self-beneficial thing to do. That is the mindful thing to do. Do not save bile as if it were fuel for the winter. The emotionally mature thing to do is to delete it.

A writer sent me an e-mail, thanking me for my books and complaining that he didn't know what to do with his novel, which was currently 200,000 words too long. I wished him luck in figuring out what he ought to do. He replied with a furious e-mail attacking me for not saying more and for not caring more. I responded that sometimes you should accept a friendly "Good luck!" in the spirit in which it is offered and get on with your life. This prompted an even longer, angrier e-mail (you know the kind, PEPPERED WITH CAPITALS), to which I didn't reply. I have no doubt that this writer was keeping himself enraged for one reason and one reason only: to avoid the hard job of revising his bloated novel. His abundant intelligence was completely subservient to his emotional immaturity.

If you embrace your bilious emotions, cherish them, take pride in them, and keep them warm by wrapping them in your immaturity, chances are that you'll find yourself making one mess after another. There you go again, agitated, angry, and upset, striding off to the liquor cabinet. Yes, you are following in the footsteps of Sinclair Lewis, Eugene O'Neill, William Faulkner, Ernest Hemingway, and John Steinbeck—all Nobel Prize winners. Or in the footsteps of Edna Saint Vincent Millay, Dorothy Parker, Djuna Barnes, and Carson McCullers. So you can take pride in that: pride in joining the pantheon of alcoholic writers.

Mind your emotions or else prepare for a gutter crawl. You think there is no cost to raging? No cost to tempests? No cost to black moods? No cost to grandiose, paranoid, histrionic—and completely unnecessary—operatic feelings? Just ask our alcoholics and suicides. Just ask anyone who lives on drama, turmoil, and bad feelings. Words such as *sanguine* and *phlegmatic* are not the most exciting words in the dictionary, but they are nevertheless golden. Become someone who is able to mind her emotions: that is an integral part of a complete mindfulness practice.

Picture a snow globe at rest and a snow globe violently shaken. Everything is the same about the two pictures, except the agitation. They are the same physical space and yet they have completely different atmospheres. In the first, ideas are available. In the second, nothing can be seen, not an idea, not the way to travel, nothing. In the first, you could get in your miniature car and drive around and arrive at your destination. In the second, you're bound to run hard into a glass wall. Calmness or emotional turmoil: which is your way?

This is not an area of your life where perfection is possible. You had high hopes that your novel would sell; it didn't; enter pain. You had high hopes that your editor would buy your second novel; she hates it; enter pain. These are not pains that are easy to shed with a little willpower, right thinking, and deep breathing. Your writing life matters to you, and it is reasonable to expect that disappointments of this sort will linger on as foul moods and a despairing outlook. But even in the face of such disasters, angle for mastery and look for the way to shorten winter.

Sometimes you may want to hold firmly on to your rage. Sometimes you may want to sink into a well-earned funk. Sometimes you may want to feel exquisitely fearful and shiver for your life. There are moments when even our darkest emotions have a place, and there are good reasons for feeling bad on occasion. But it is not a healthy way of life. Limit your darker emotions just as you limit your intake of chocolate: just like a little sweet, a little sour goes a long way.

LESSON 15

An emotionally intelligent, emotionally mature person does not strive to avoid feeling and does not hope against hope that unwanted feelings will stop arising. Rather, he monitors his emotions and masters them by embracing the ones he wants and discarding the ones he doesn't. This isn't an easy practice, but it is an invaluable one.

To Do

1. The next time you get angry, decide not to be angry.
2. The next time you get morose, decide not to be morose.
3. The next time you get envious, decide not to be envious.
4. The next time you experience any emotion, embrace it or discard it: your choice.

CHAPTER 16

The Weight of Individuality

Jt is a creative person's individuality that defines him. Most people are conventional and prize conformity; some people prize their individuality. Even if he trains himself to hold his tongue, an individual will already know as a young child that he can't conform and that he wasn't built to conform. Looking around, unable to understand why people are acting so conventionally, starting to feel alienated, out of place, and like a "stranger in a strange land," he finds himself burdened by this pulsing energy: the fierce need to be himself. This need produces lifelong emotional consequences.

If you are born individual and find yourself presented with some arbitrary, odd-sounding rule—that you can only play with one of your toys at a time or that God will be offended if you don't wear a hat—you immediately ask "Why?" If the answer makes no sense to you or if you get your ears boxed, you cry

"No!" and begin to grow oppositional. A certain oppositional attitude naturally and inevitably flows from an individual's adamant effort to reject humbug and to make personal sense of the world. What does this feel like, emotionally? It feels like a combination of sorrow and anger, tangled together to form a root ball of depression.

This oppositional attitude, perhaps suppressed in childhood, begins to announce itself and assert itself in adolescence and to grow as an individual's interactions with the conventional world increase. It grows as his ability to "do his thing" is directly or indirectly restricted by the machinery of society. He finds himself in an odd kind of fight, not necessarily with any particular person or group of people but with everyone and everything meant to constrain him and reduce him to a cipher. He finds himself in a fight to the death, a fight to retain his individuality.

One proof that this dynamic actually takes place is the frequency with which we see it in the lives of creative people. Arnold Ludwig, in his study of "1000 extraordinary men and women" called *The Price of Greatness*, explained: "These individuals often have an attitude set that is oppositional in nature. These are not people who just see that the emperor has no clothes; they offer their own brand of attire for him to wear."

Popping out of the womb individual, needing to experiment and to risk as part of their individuality, and feeling thwarted and frustrated by the oh-so-conventional universe into which they have been plopped at birth, the world's individuals rush headlong like a ski jumper down a ramp toward reckless ways of dealing with their feelings of alienation and frustration. They are not only individual, they are driven to be individual, a drive that sets them apart and sends them racing through life.

Nature is not stupid. Nature makes the calculation that, for an individual to truly be individual, it had better invest him with enough power, passion, energy, and appetite to manifest that individuality. Otherwise individuality would be a cosmic joke, and nature doesn't joke that way. So it invests the individual with extra drive. Just as it makes no sense to produce a creature that enjoys the leaves at the tops of trees without also providing him with a long neck, it makes no sense to produce a creature that is built to assert his individuality without providing him with the energy of assertion. This nature does.

Thus the individual has more energy, more charisma, bigger appetites, stronger needs, greater passion, more aliveness, more avidity: this is all the same idea and flows from the same well-spring. It is nature's way of fueling the individual so that he can be individual. It should also be clear how this extra energy and fuller appetite lead to conditions such as addiction, mania, and insatiability.

Nature does not joke, but it does produce unintended consequences. One of the major unfortunate consequences of this extra drive—this extra ambition, this extra egotism, this extra appetite—is that the individual is hard-pressed, and often completely unable, to feel satisfied.

He eats a hundred peanuts—not satisfying enough. He writes a good book—not satisfying enough. He has a shot of excellent Scotch—not satisfying enough. He wins the Nobel Prize—not satisfying enough. This inability to get satisfied produces constant background unhappiness and makes him want some experience that will mask this feeling or make it go away. So he has another hundred peanuts or another Scotch—without, however, coming any closer to satisfying himself.

It is as if nature turbocharged some of its creatures and then failed to give them a decent braking system. It provided extra energy—and with it a susceptibility to mania. It provided extra ambition—and with it a susceptibility to grandiosity. It provided extra appetite—and with it a susceptibility to promiscuity, obesity, and alcoholism. It provided extra adrenaline—and with it a susceptibility to car wrecks. If all of these "extras" could be channeled and regulated, we might thank nature for its largesse. As it is, these extras make the individual's life unruly and fraught with danger.

So nature, which doesn't joke, nevertheless has its little joke and creates an individual who must know for himself, follow his own path, and be himself, puts it in his mind that he is born to do earth-shattering and life-saving work, gives him the energy to pursue this work and the courage to stand in opposition even to the whole world, and then turns around and tortures him. It heightens his core anxiety by giving him an existential outlook, making sure that nothing will satisfy him, pouring adrenaline through his system, and swelling his head so that he is primed to tip over, top-heavy, into self-centeredness.

The mandate to individuality forces the creative person to wonder about life's large questions—pesters him with those questions—and demands that he respond to what he sees going on in the universe. It forces him to write a mournful poem, craft a subversive novel, and walk the earth from one end to the other on some unnameable quest. Each of these is an existential response, that is, a response arising from his plaintive, poignant questioning of the world into which nature has dropped him. On top of everything else, nature tells him that he is responsible for looking out for the world—nothing less is expected of him.

Of course, we aren't equal to all of this. As individual as we are, as magnificent as we are, we are also quite puny. We may be large, but we are also small. Even if we do manage to persevere—

to write our poems, to battle our windmills—it is not without a thousand ups and downs, frustrations and disappointments, rages and dirges. Is this your emotional landscape? Then you are probably an individual.

LESSON 16

Individuality has emotional consequences. Nature may have designated you as one of her individuals, but she has not provided you with a blueprint to follow. You will have to work that out, even while nursing a pain in your heart and a pain in your head.

To Do

1. Be the individual that you are. Do you really have a choice?
2. Become more mindful of your emotional landscape by adopting a self-observer's attitude. Rage against injustice, but also observe what that rage is doing to your system. Write manically, but also observe whether you are racing too fast. Monitor yourself—that is your duty.
3. Learn how to calm yourself through the practice of slow, deep breathing. You have no better soothing tool than the regulation of your own breathing; use it to counteract your inner turmoil and speediness.
4. Wear the weight of your individuality as lightly as you can.

CHAPTER 17

Quick Centering

Y ou can learn to center and quiet your mind and your emotions by taking ten-second pauses of the sort that I'm about to describe. You may be amazed to learn that a truly life-altering strategy can come in a package as small as ten seconds, but it can. This simple technique has two components, a breathing part and a thinking part. First you practice deep breathing until you can produce a breath that lasts about five seconds on the inhale and five seconds on the exhale. Then you insert a thought into the breath, silently thinking half the thought on the inhale and half the thought on the exhale. That's it.

This sounds very simple, and it is. This ten-second centering technique is simple to grasp, simple to use, and simple to master. It's nevertheless profound in its benefits. You will be able to do things that previously felt too painful or too difficult to attempt. You will be able to calm and center yourself before you write.

You will change your basic attitudes about life, moving from pessimism to optimism, procrastination to effort, and worry to calm. These are the benefits that await you. (For a full discussion of this technique and its benefits, please take a look at my book *Ten Zen Seconds*.)

The first thing I'd like you to do is familiarize yourself with what ten seconds feel like. Look at the second hand of your watch and experience ten seconds. What I think you'll notice is that ten seconds is a surprisingly long amount of time. It probably feels longer and more substantial than you expected it would. Each second of the ten seconds is a distinct entity, clearly separate and distinguishable from the one that preceded it and the one that followed it. Doesn't a full ten seconds feel like a small lifetime?

The customary breath you take is on the order of two or three seconds in duration. This is normal, natural, automatic, and does a fine job of keeping you alive. Exactly because it is natural and automatic, a breath of this length does nothing to interrupt your mind chatter or to alter your sense of a given situation. When you consciously decide to breathe more slowly and deeply, you alert your body to the fact that something is up and that you want it to behave differently.

This long, deep breath serves as a container for specific thoughts. Before it does that, however, it serves as the best way available to you to stop and address what you are doing and thinking. If you've been doing something compulsive and harmful to yourself, this alteration in breathing gives you the chance to become aware of your behavior. If you've been obsessively worrying about something, the conscious production of one long, deep breath interrupts your mind flow and provides you with a golden opportunity to counter your anxious thoughts. A long, deep breath is the equivalent of a full stop and the key to centering.

You may want to build up to your long, deep breath with several preliminary breaths that you use to progressively deepen your breathing pattern. I predict that ultimately you will find this unnecessary and that you will be able to switch from your ordinary breathing-and-thinking pattern to your centering incantations from one breath to the next. For now, if it helps you to arrive at a long, deep breath by progressively breathing more deeply, by all means allow yourself as many warm-up breaths as you need.

The meat of this technique is using the deep breath that you just mastered as a container to hold a specific thought. Let's consider two different thoughts: "stained glass window" and "I am perfectly fine." When you insert a thought into a long, deep breath, you need to decide how to break the thought up so that it divides naturally and rhythmically between the inhale and the exhale. You'll discover, for instance, that "stained glass window" divides most naturally as (stained glass) and (window) and "I am perfectly fine" divides most naturally as (I am perfectly) and (fine). Give this a try and see if you agree.

Now we're ready to look at the specific thoughts I suggest you "drop into" your long, deep breaths. I'll use parentheses to indicate how these phrases (or incantations, as I call them) naturally divide. Notice that Incantation Three functions differently from the other eleven. It is a "name your work" incantation. You think something different each time you employ it, depending on the work you intend to accomplish. For instance, if your work is your current novel, your phrase might be (I am ready) (to write) or (I am tackling) (this chapter). I'm using (I am) (doing my work) as a place-marker to stand for the idea that you name specific work each time you use this incantation.

Here are the twelve incantations:

1. (I am completely) (stopping)
2. (I expect) (nothing)
3. (I am) (doing my work)
4. (I trust) (my resources)
5. (I feel) (supported)
6. (I embrace) (this moment)
7. (I am free) (of the past)
8. (I make) (my meaning)
9. (I am open) (to joy)

10. (I am equal) (to this challenge)
11. (I am) (taking action)
12. (I return) (with strength)

Try out these twelve incantations right now. Take the time to go through the list slowly, incorporating each phrase into its own long, deep breath. Begin with some preparatory centering breaths, breathe-and-think the first thought "(I am completely) (stopping)," and pause before moving on to the next incantation. Take your time and begin to experience the power of these twelve phrases.

Each of these phrases has its purpose and logic. I expect that you've already grasped what each incantation is intended to do. When you first enter your writing space, try out "I am completely stopping." When you doubt that you are equal to writing your current screenplay, try out "I trust my resources." When you get into a black mood about needing to send out another round of query e-mails to literary agents, try out "I am equal to this challenge." When your mind inadvertently lands on that criticism you received at the hands of your third-grade teacher, try out "I am free of the past." You will find that one or another of these twelve thoughts is exactly the right thought to cleanse and center you in any situation.

Traditional centering techniques require time—a half-hour listening to a relaxation tape, fifteen minutes going through postures, twenty minutes quieting mind chatter. More tellingly, they have no thought component. They help you relax, focus your mind, and calm your nerves, but they do not provide you with a repertoire of useful thoughts to meet the real challenges that you face. Lucinda, a writer from Milwaukee, complained: "I've tried many things but nothing seems to keep me focused. Sometimes I feel that being centered is something that just happens to a fortunate few while the rest of us are doomed to wander around in a daze." This may have been your experience; now you have something to try.

Whether you use the phrases that I've provided, each of which has a certain rationale, or phrases of your own creation, I hope that you will make ten-second centering an integral part of your program to manage your moods and your mind. The marrying of a deep breath with a useful thought is simplicity itself. Get into the habit of breathing-and-thinking "I am equal to this challenge," "I trust my resources," or your favorite incantation as you get ready to write, when you feel distracted, or any time you want to deepen your experience of the moment.

LESSON 17

Learn to center quickly. You could spend hours each day getting ready to write—or ten seconds. Which seems more advantageous and economical?

To Do

1. Practice these twelve incantations.
2. Create some of your own.
3. Use them.
4. Turn them into an enduring habit.

Chapter 18

Upgrading Your Personality

You won't live a happy, productive writing life if your writing room is tidy and you are a mess. Honoring your writing means, in addition to everything else that it means, upgrading your personality. You want to become someone who is less chaotic, more confident, less distractible, more motivated, less defensive, and so on. Of course you can enter your writing space as a burned-out case and still manage to get words on the page, but they are unlikely to be your best ones and they may be among your last ones.

Two of our greatest playwrights, Tennessee Williams and Arthur Miller, very different in outlook, temperament, and orientation, shared a common history: excellent work early on, poorer work later on. This is a typical story, especially for American writers. Many writers manage to put words on the page, decade after decade, and yet aren't really present at their handsome desk in their splendid workspace. The shadows in their personality, shadows that have grown darker over time, cast a pall over everything and their current writing is a mere shadow of their former writing.

It turns out that if we do not upgrade our personality, it tends to degrade. Our depressions start taking a bigger toll, our addictions begin to win, our imaginative powers start to wither, our output dwindles, our isolation increases, our despair deepens. Maybe we started out with certain cravings and a charming, zany, unhinged way of being; with each failed relationship and whiff of mortality, each round of excess and recurrent bad dream, we decline further.

Imagine that you are the following person. You are thirty-two years old, single, white, female. You have a degree in English and two half-miserable European trips, seven tumultuous love affairs, and a rocky draft of a novel to your credit. You are very busy—text messaging, checking e-mails, working a job, running by the reservoir, collecting information about how to store the good Bordeaux and why dating a married man might make sense—but, as busy as you are, you feel as if you're sleepwalking. You say to yourself, "If I could just get that damned novel revised or maybe start a second one, maybe that would help." What you don't say is "I need a personality upgrade."

You know that it's rare for you to have a complete thought, a complete feeling, or a sense of completeness about anything nowadays. You have a lot of eggs left but not so many that each period isn't meaningful. You wish that you could build a little Zen garden and sit there and be quiet and have that change everything, but you've tried that, or something like that, and it gave you the kind of headache that Tylenol couldn't touch. Oh, you look whole enough and you can fool bus drivers and your therapist, who keeps cheering you on to nowhere. But you know that you need something and you say to yourself, "Maybe I'll try a dating service." What you don't say is "I need a personality upgrade."

You meant to write more than the first draft of one novel. You can taste the books you were meant to write, smell the sea air of this one, and feel the knife's edge of that one. But you are very far away from writing them. You are thirty-two, single, white, female, and something happened, something that can't be captured in a journal entry or corrected with laser surgery. Somewhere you lost something: your balance, your dream, your wherewithal. But it doesn't occur to you to announce "I need a personality upgrade."

That is exactly what you need. You do it in the following way, by selecting three or four qualities from the master list of qualities that life provides and by producing a simple sentence of the following sort: "I intend to live a calmer, more disciplined, more thoughtful life." Or: "I intend to live a more passionate, more productive, more present life." Or: "I intend to live a life that's more generous and more ambitious." Next, you turn your excellent sentence into concrete actions. You do something generous. You tackle something ambitious. You start a meditation practice to support your desire to grow calmer. You write every day, to honor your new goal of increased discipline.

This is simplicity itself: name what you want from yourself, then take action. "I want to sit still for a whole Sunday and really begin my next novel." Beautiful: you sit still for a whole Sunday and begin your novel. "I want to stop feeling anxious and inferior, so I'm going to learn some deep-breathing techniques and I'm going to release every ounce of my inferiority complex." Beautiful: you breathe deeply, let inferiority evaporate from your skin, and write from a place of worthiness. "I want to stop being such a drama king and narcissist, so I'm going to go a full week without drama and without preening." Beautiful: you wake up on Monday, begin your screenplay, and when, after fifteen minutes, you don't know what to write next, you refuse to make a mini-drama out of your situation. Instead, you just keep going.

Of course it can't be as simple as this. I am completely fibbing by claiming that you can upgrade your personality by crafting a useful sentence and taking some action. And yet . . . who knows? What can you lose by giving it a try?

LESSON 18

Figure out what you want from yourself, not what you want for yourself. Head in that direction.

To Do

1. Describe the upgraded personality you want.
2. Name the actions corresponding to that vision.
3. Take those actions.
4. Become that person.

Part V

Reflective Space

CHAPTER 19

Mindful Self-Reflection

Mindful self-reflection is the "space" we enter when we want to make productive changes, better understand what we want for our creative life, and guarantee that we are keeping an eye on our goals. It is different from mere unproductive worry and has, as its emotional component, a calmness that results from our practiced way of breathing through anxiety, quieting our mind and honoring our dreams.

Mindful self-reflection is a crucial ingredient in our recipe for living a creative life. Where does our next novel come from? Not from the cupboard or the closet. It comes from a way of being that invites its arrival. We are its container, its host, and its messenger. If we are doing the sorts of prophylactic things that ensure that it will not be birthed, we are the one practicing birth control on our own creativity.

Take Louise. A woman in her late forties, Louise had carved out a life for herself as a midwife to women writers. She led groups, workshops, and retreats for women, helped them open up and tell their stories, often for the first time, and for the last five years had even been able to earn a living from this work, albeit a meager one. Still, although she knew that she was performing a valuable service, a serious inner conflict remained.

She wasn't doing any of her own writing, which made her feel incomplete. She couldn't help but agree with her parents and her siblings, who, highly successful in their professions, wondered why Louise had accomplished so little, given her excellent education and her abundant talents. Wasn't Louise supposed to lead as well as serve, create as well as midwife the creations of others, be in better financial shape, and make more of her life? She couldn't quite say whether these were her own ideas, her family's ideas, or ideas embedded in the culture, but she knew that she was carrying around a deep sense of failure.

She started her mindfulness practice with the question, "Am I really a writer?" This was a painful question to address because it seemed as if there could be no good answer. If it came to her that she wasn't a writer, that would feel terrible; and if it came to her that she was a writer, that would confirm her intuition that she'd failed herself. She didn't know what she could possibly gain by contemplating this question, and she began her practice a little mournfully, as many people who opt for self-awareness do.

For several consecutive nights she had vivid dreams, most of them involving forests at night. It was as if she'd been dropped into a fairy-tale world out of the Brothers Grimm, a world of lost children in woolen leggings, wood nymphs, and princes disguised as wolves and princesses disguised as swans. These scenes, however, had nothing to say to her. It was somehow not very different from spending the night at the opera or the ballet.

She tried a new question: "If I were to write, what would I write?" The same dreams returned. Only now the forest creatures kept changing their identities and their gender. Sometimes the wolves were princes and sometimes they morphed into princesses. The same happened with the swans, the squirrels, the deer, and the snakes. With each dream she saw this more clearly, until, in one dream, she observed all the forest creatures change before her eyes in rapid succession, a wolf transforming itself from prince to swan to princess to squirrel, morphing again and again.

When she woke up she discovered that she had learned something: she didn't have to be just one sort of creature; she, too, could morph and change. She realized that she had two tasks to perform, affirming the appropriateness of her work as midwife while at the same time letting her own stories out. She'd always known this, but before she'd held the matter as an either/or proposition. For some reason it had seemed that she had to either serve or lead—she couldn't do both. Now she wondered why on earth she'd ever thought that.

On second thought, she knew why: in the world in which she grew up, girls became nurses and boys became doctors. Girls got comfortable with bedpans and boys were sent out to be the visionaries. It suddenly struck her as strange that she had gotten this cultural message even though, in her own family, the girls had been given an equal shot at education and had been encouraged to excel. Still, there was some hum in the background, some undercurrent, some way in which the boys got more privileges or maybe just experienced the world in a more privileged way. That hum must have affected her. She had never been told, "Help others; don't do your own work," and yet somewhere, somehow she had gotten that message.

Now she saw that she needed just to be herself, freed from that piece of unconscious bondage. Instantly she knew what she wanted to write about: her experiences in India leading writing workshops for untouchable women. She had gone to India five times and had spent almost a year there altogether. For the longest time she'd known that she should tell the story of her experiences there, what her Indian students had taught her and what she had taught them, intermingled with the sights, smells, and colors of India. It would make for a fascinating and revealing book, if only she could write it.

Was she ready? Was it too late for her to begin her life as a writer? She answered the first question in the affirmative and the second in the negative and posed herself a new, beautiful question: "How should my Indian story begin?" Instead of waiting for an answer, she took herself right to the computer and, without any idea of what to expect and without knowing where to begin, she waited, surprisingly calmly, as her computer booted up.

In the time that it took for her computer to boot up, she heard herself think, "If I do not reflect on my life in this deep way, I get amazingly stuck, so stuck that I don't do my own creative work. In order to write, I have to enter into a certain kind of self-relationship, not that of a cheerleader or a taskmaster but a private investigator, someone who has taken my case, someone who is willing to look at the evidence and hunt for clues. I've always said that life was a mystery. I don't think that I understood that it required a real detective!"

You are the mystery; and you are the detective. Begin your practice of mindful self-reflection.

LESSON 19

We make many kinds of spaces for ourselves: noisy spaces, busy spaces, unsettled spaces, and sometimes calm self-reflective spaces. Make a calm self-reflective space for yourself by growing quiet. Then consider what your writing life needs—and how you'll meet those needs.

To Do

1. Grow quiet.
2. Reflect.
3. Stay calm.
4. Take action.

CHAPTER 20

Making Space for Seville

Joyce was a successful magazine editor who, when she came to see me, had just celebrated her sixtieth birthday. Over the years her creativity had manifested itself in picking and editing articles for the magazine, choosing covers, and doing all of the other things that came with her job. That was a full-time job and more.

Joyce also kept to a strict exercise regimen, did early morning yoga, and served on the board of an organization that raised money for dancers with AIDS. She gave parties, traveled with her husband, planned vacations with her grown children, and mentored young editors at work, some of whom had gone on to successful careers at other magazines.

Yet all of this was not enough. For the longest time she had wanted to write a historical novel set in medieval Seville. The setting was crystal clear, and she had some characters and some plot in mind. But she had never started the novel, not even to jot down a few notes. It seemed that a wall stood between her and beginning her book. Each time she thought about the novel, she reminded herself that she was very busy and that each of the things she was doing was valuable in its own right. While that was undeniably true, she nevertheless felt as if she were failing herself.

For more than forty years she had wanted to do some writing and the fact that she had never given it a chance deeply disappointed her. We discussed reducing her commitments and even dropping a few of them and starting each day writing her novel, rather than in her usual way with yoga, exercise, and journaling. She agreed in a lukewarm way to my suggestions and also agreed to reflect on the question: "Where does my writing fit in?"

The thought that popped into her mind the next morning was, "All right, first thing." She took that to mean that she should start each day writing her novel. But she couldn't pull the feat off. She exercised instead. The morning after that she had pressing reasons to get to the office early. The third morning she simply dismissed the idea that she could start right in writing. Every morning she woke up thinking about writing her novel, but on no morning did she do any writing. By the end of the week she found herself in a foul mood.

At our next session I wondered what other reflective questioning she might try. She didn't seem inclined to engage in self-reflection or motivated to discover what might be preventing her from writing. But finally she agreed to try another week of mindful reflection, this time using the prompt "medieval Seville." I wanted her to think about her book, not about writing or not writing, and the phrase "medieval Seville" seemed promising as a door opener.

Over the next several days she found herself sometimes muttering the phrase "medieval Seville." A couple of times she caught herself completely stopped, unaware of her surroundings, not checking items off her mental to-do list but lost in the medieval Seville that her imagination was creating. She knew that something was shifting inside of her, although she still hadn't written a word.

On the fifth day she stole a few minutes during the afternoon between meetings to jot down some notes about the Seville she was envisioning. She saw the narrow back streets . . . and a single snarling dog . . . which put her in mind of bull runs . . . which in turn caused her to picture a runaway bull on a dark, moonless night. She wrote her thoughts down.

These were the first actual bits of writing on the book that she had ever managed. The next morning she woke up and went right to the computer. She began describing the wild bull, the moonless night, the narrow streets, and her heroine, who all of a sudden came to her. She wrote for an hour and then had to rush to make it to work for a meeting. But even as she rushed she found that she was still thinking about her embryonic novel. She understood that this morning marked a real breakthrough.

She also understood that unless she made self-reflection a daily practice, her writing life might slip away again. The practice she instituted involved letting go of and mourning several of her previous activities (a few of which, once she let them go, she didn't miss or mourn all that much), changing her relationship to the magazine, which she still oversaw but with a less consuming intensity, and consciously getting to her writing first thing each morning for at least an hour, even on the weekends.

It was not a smooth ride to the first draft of her novel. There were many days when she felt pulled in too many directions, many days when she found herself hating the draft and wondering why she was putting herself through this torture, many days when it upset her that the magazine looked to be a slipping a little. But finally the draft was done: a much less beautiful thing than she hoped it would be but full of potential. She knew exactly what she needed to do next: to enter her "reflective space" and commit to honorably revising the draft, once, twice, as many times as necessary.

LESSON 20

You have a coach available to help you reflect on your writing life, improve your writing life, and make sure that you maintain a writing life. That coach is you. Whenever you need some writing advice, enter a "reflective space" and coach yourself to your own best answers.

To Do

1. Name a challenge in your writing life.
2. Reflect on the question "How can I handle this challenge?"
3. Open up to your own solutions.
4. Choose one to implement.

CHAPTER 21

Frank and Janet

Frank had grown up with critical parents who made him feel worthless. If he played a piano piece decently, they commented on the way he'd slouched, how shy he'd seemed, or how much better they'd expected him to play considering all the lessons he'd taken. If he ate all the food on his plate, they wondered if he was trying to fatten himself up; if he left food over, they wondered if he knew how much a year's worth of groceries cost. Nothing he did pleased them.

The upshot of their meanness was to ruin his ability to freely make mistakes. He still made mistakes, since we all do, but he hated them and tried to hide them from himself and from everyone else. As he couldn't really hide them, he ended up chastising himself and saying things like "Only a champion idiot like me could make this many mistakes."

Finally he realized that he had to change his attitude, since his fear of mistakes was ruining his ability to write decent papers in his graduate psychology program. Because he felt that he needed perfect, complete knowledge of his subject before starting a paper, he invariably delayed starting them; then, at the last minute, he would grind something inferior out. What he produced was never as good as the paper he might have written if he had felt free to write multiple drafts.

Desperate, he agreed to engage in some mindful self-reflection, using the question "What can I do about my fear of mistakes?" as his starting point. For a few days nothing came to him even though he sat quietly for fifteen minutes twice a day and tried to open up to answers. Then one night he had a dream about mud, the kind of mud you make when you're painting a picture and mix too many pigments together. It was a dream about painter's mud.

What he saw in his dream was a happy child obliviously mixing pigments together, making a face at the mud he produced, and blithely starting over. The child in the dream just didn't care that he had wasted some paint. It wasn't a tragedy or any sort of issue at all. No word like "mistake," "failure," "stupid," "wasteful," or "incompetent" crossed the little boy's mind. He made some mud, discarded it, and started over, as happy as a lark. Frank realized that he wanted to live his life exactly that way.

He made the pledge to himself that he would learn to live like that little boy, like the person he might have been if he hadn't received so much disabling criticism. His mantra became "mud means nothing." He began to freely write without worrying that maybe he didn't know enough, that maybe somebody had already said what he was thinking of saying, or that maybe he had no profound insights to share. By focusing on one issue, his lifelong fear of making mistakes and messes, he altered the course of his writing life.

Janet's circumstances were different. She had raised two children with her husband, Mark, with whom she had a decent if distant relationship. Their children looked successful, getting good grades in school and participating in all sorts of extracurricular activities. Their daughter, Elizabeth, was an excellent tennis player and their son, Alex, was his soccer team's star forward, and from the outside everything about Janet's family life looked ideal. But Janet, who worked outside the home at a large company and who chalked up her inability to write to the fact that she had no time for writing, was still suffering in her early forties from a trauma that dated back to her late teens.

Before Mark there had been another man in Janet's life. During that relationship Janet had become pregnant, had had their baby, and had given it up for adoption. Ever since, the abiding messages in Janet's brain were "I'm evil" and "I don't deserve to have anything good happen to me." She believed that her self-hatred had led to self-censorship and prevented her from writing. At the same time, she wondered if giving up her child had anything to do with her writing block, and whether dwelling on the event was the actual problem. As she was of two minds about the matter, she'd decided that she would just not think about it at all.

Still, she agreed to practice a little mindful self-reflection, despite the intensely painful nature of the issue. Several weeks later she informed me that she had decided to look for her son and to write about the search. I asked her how she'd come to that conclusion. She replied that, through some process of softening and surrender that she couldn't put into words, an opening had occurred; and through that opening a dream had arrived.

It was a dream about a therapy session in which she was the client and her son, all grown up, was the therapist. What was most important about the dream experience was that her son didn't seem to hate her. She couldn't really hear what they were saying but she could tell by the way he sometimes smiled and by his general demeanor that, although he was asking her tough questions, he wasn't being critical of her. By the end of the dream she knew that she wanted to find him.

She grudgingly admitted that burying the experience of giving up her child for adoption had probably tied her in knots and prevented her from writing. She wished that she'd forthrightly faced the matter years sooner and not squandered so much time avoiding the issue; but at least she was facing it now, and with something like equanimity. She announced that she was ready to feel whatever she was in store to feel and to record that journey in writing.

We may have experienced things, such as persistent criticism or repeated rejection, that now prevent us from writing. We may have done things, such as inflicted harm or wreaked havoc, that stop us from writing. As painful and difficult as it may be to face those issues, can we write if we don't face them? The answer is: hard to say. Sometimes we overcome such difficulties by committing to our writing practice and by showing up every day at our computer. Sometimes we have to engage in self-reflection and experience healing before we can move forward.

LESSON 21

Commit to writing or commit to reflecting on what is stopping you from writing. Do one or the other.

To Do

1. Make a list of the issues that prevent you from writing. Don't force issues onto the list, but at the same time be open and give issues a chance to surface.

2. Reflect on your list. If an issue stands out, address it.
3. Even before you have it completely resolved, say to yourself, "I think I'll write anyway." See if you can get on with your writing at the same time that you are dealing with the issues in your life.
4. If an issue seems intractable, seek help.

Part VI

Imagined Space

CHAPTER 22

Desiring Worlds into Existence

F ront and center in our genetic memory is the experience of worlds arising out of solar explosions. Some worlds, such as Mercury, were made very hot; some, such as Jupiter, were made very cold. Some, such as our Earth, gave rise to apple orchards, mosquitoes, and us. As part of our genetic understanding, we know all about the creation of countless dead worlds and the creation of occasional beautiful, meaningful, and coherent worlds—and we know which we prefer.

Because of that genetic understanding, we feel a peculiar pressure to replicate existence and create beautiful, meaningful, coherent worlds of our own. We see that, out of nothing much, just strings and process, our own world got made. Desire bubbling up from our depths gets us hungry to make a world too. Creating such a world feels like the best use of our time on Earth and even seduces us into feeling like the creator of (a/the) whole universe. We say, "I can build worlds too! Bring it on!"

So we begin. A first step in creating this new world is to collect matter, as even gods need matter in order to make their visions manifest. Our matter is composed of ideas, images, feelings, and punctuation. But those are the molecules of our world, not its fundamental particles. Even more fundamental is our desire to create. A subatomic entity such as a string is driven energy; so is our writing. Our writing is made of sentences that desire alone has created.

The instant our desire fails, so do our world-building efforts. When our desire returns, we find ourselves once again at play in the fields of words. Can you cause a fictional 1890s Boise to materialize without a real desire to do so? Not even a god could. Focus on desire, then! If you focus on desire, you will be keeping your eye on the fountainhead.

It doesn't matter what problem you're encountering with your writing: focus on the rekindling of desire. If the problem is that a character is flat, rekindle your desire to breathe life into him. If the problem is that it's time to write a synopsis of your novel and the absurdity of that task demoralizes you, rekindle your desire to present your world to the public. If the problem is that Chapter 3 is excellent and that Chapter 4 is dull, rekindle your desire to make Chapter 4 worthy.

A client of mine confessed: "I reflect on my own process and I realize that for a long time I've been playing it quasi-Zen-cool, trying very hard to start my engines without kindling any sparks of desire. Inevitably this leads to inconsistent efforts. I've had maybe one or two spurts of activity, followed by long lulls. Probably this stems from a lack of respect for my own work, as I go about coolly treating everything as practice, everything as a study, so that I don't have to deal with the fact that the work might just suck. This cool, non-stick Teflon method has worked all too well: I've managed to throw the baby out with the bathwater. I understand now that this Teflon method doesn't raise any stakes for me. There is no commitment, hence no risk. Work can't be created without intention, without desire."

Mere motivation isn't enough. We think that our life would make a good story—that amounts to mere motivation. We think the subject we've been teaching for years would make for a good nonfiction book—that amounts to mere motivation. That sort of motivation peters out at the first signs of difficulty: that is, somewhere on the first page. If we are not burning to create, our chances of actually creating are slight. Do not be afraid to burn hot in the service of your work! Get excited, worked up, a little manic. Zen cool is cool; but dharma teachers tend not to get much writing done.

Writers who write are dancing bundles of desire. They crave sex, peanuts, and Nobel Prizes. They crave; they itch; they lust; they are alive. Whether they effectively manage their abundant desires is a separate question, but without all that dancing, pressing desire they'd sit quietly like old folks lined up in the corridor of a nursing home. Honor your goal to create new worlds by burning with desire. Be incandescent—or else nothing will happen.

Here is a little creation ditty, a creator's Babylonian Genesis:

I am a world-builder.
That isn't so easy.
But I am a world-builder.
Despite all my disabilities.
I am a world-builder.
Desire is the complete prescription.
Whether I find myself at stage one of my book, stage two, or anywhere along the Tao.
Without desire I am done.
Every day I rekindle my desire. Somehow.
Hallelujah.

LESSON 22

In the space where imagining happens, worlds arise if you kindle your desire. Do not be so cool, detached, and phlegmatic that you starve yourself and your art. Burn! In the light of that flame you will see sights worth describing.

To Do

1. Want. That's okay.
2. Really want. That's really okay.
3. Have you been hungering for years to write a certain piece while simultaneously curbing your enthusiasm and, by curbing it, killing it? Set the table. Light some candles. Get out the good china. Serve up your delicious piece to yourself, no enthusiasm spared.
4. Can't locate your desire? It may be buried under a hundred doubts and disappointments. Train a flashlight in that direction—no, a spotlight.

CHAPTER 23

Setting as Big Idea

Y ou inhabit many spaces: your mental space, your emotional space, your physical space. Then there are the spaces you inhabit when you write: the setting of your novel, the milieu of your nonfiction book, the geography of your poem. You inhabit an imagined Rome, imagined fields blazing under an imagined sun, an imagined sea and imagined ships. Then, when it's your readers' turn, they inhabit these imagined spaces too.

I grew up in Brooklyn. I can picture the Brooklyn of my youth with photographic clarity. But I can also picture with equal clarity places I have only visited as a reader: the Algeria of Albert Camus's childhood as described in *The First Man*, the pastoral England of Thomas Hardy, the New England whaling world of Herman Melville, the southern small-town world of Harper Lee's *To Kill a Mockingbird*. The richness of these settings is a gift to readers. We not only get to travel in our imagination but we are helped to fathom what we want our life to mean.

By inhabiting an author's Saint Petersburg, Paris, or Savannah for a few hours, we rework our understanding of the universe. We augment our understanding of class and privilege as we watch tea served from a silver samovar. We change our mind about how much personal space we need as we live with a character in her under-the-eaves Paris studio. We recalibrate our conception of race relations as we attend an all-white private club luncheon waited on by an all-black wait staff. We are not in "the real" Saint Petersburg, Paris, or Savannah: we are in a place the author has created, learning what the author intended us to learn.

This is imagined space: setting as big idea, as big as character, plot, or theme. The setting of a piece of writing, whether in fiction or nonfiction, is never a comprehensive snapshot of a place. If you tried to describe with the utmost accuracy every structure in a city—every hovel, every mansion, every shop, every government building—and went on to describe every stitch of clothing, every banquet, every parade, you wouldn't capture anything essential about that place. We wouldn't know what it felt like to be an abstract painter in Greenwich Village in the Forties or, further uptown, a young girl growing up during the Harlem Renaissance. No catalogue can do that work: we need an author's art and intentions.

Just as you have an intention for the physical space in which you work, that you write deeply there, so you conjure intentions for the spaces you write into existence. Maybe you picture a place—Berlin, an oasis in the desert, or your small town in the Midwest—and hear yourself say, "I could communicate something about the way this place has changed and, by doing that, get at how the world has changed." Or: "I could communicate something about the way this place has remained the same and in that way get at how nothing really changes." Isn't that more interesting than picturing monuments and museums?

You might think, "Maybe I could explore why I am so (happy, sad, excited, bored, restless, thrilled, despairing, ecstatic) when I visit this place." Or: "Maybe I can get at my thoughts about (culture, spirituality, history, my family, my childhood) using this place as a metaphor or container." Or: "Wouldn't it be interesting to explore the profound subject of (evolution, race relations, postmodern vacuum) using this place as a backdrop?" These excellent intentions produce fascinating settings.

Let your rendering of place follow your intentions. If your intention is to communicate your ideas about contemporary culture set against the backdrop of Paris, you use Paris differently than if your intention is to tell the story of two lovers in the Marais, or a homeless family in Belleville, or a jewel heist in the Place Vendôme. In each case we will see a different Paris, one drawn from the real and from the imagined and designed to serve your intentions.

Setting is not just the place where things happen: it helps define what can happen. It is part of the very idea. These imagined spaces, fashioned from reality but no more real than the settings in dreams, do not exist for any reason except to serve an author's intentions.

LESSON 23

Hold setting as a big idea, as big as character, plot, theme, or any aspect of the writer's craft.

To Do

1. You've been given a freelance assignment to write about an imaginary city. The city is presented to you in an odd way, fact by fact. Take each fact as it's presented and see what thoughts and feelings arise in you.
   - It is a city of three million people.
   - The city's main industry is the manufacture of toys.
   - The city's history goes back two thousand years.
   - A river runs through the middle of the city.
   - Its buildings are made of wood.
   - They are painted bright colors.

- Every building in the city sports a crest.
- The people of this city communicate by gesturing with their left hand.
- It is a tourist destination, but only for tourists who are charmed by people who gesture but do not speak.

Build an imaginary place, fact by fact, that serves one of your writing intentions.

2. Answer the following question: How does "place" work in a piece of nonfiction where there is no apparent setting?

3. Pick a place that interests you or that you are considering using in some way. Then do the following:

- Name ten things you find surprising or unique about your place.
- Describe ten specific sights there.
- Describe ten local characters or character types.
- Name ten interesting ideas that you would like to examine using your place as a vehicle or backdrop.

4. Dream up a themed collection of essays held together by setting.

CHAPTER 24

Sitting on Keats's Bench

Hampstead is a posh North London village-feeling neighborhood that boasts Hampstead Heath, fine churches, finer mansions, offbeat theater, the requisite upscale restaurants, pubs, markets, and boutiques, and, on Keats Place, Keats's idyllic house, in actuality two Regency cottages combined into one well-visited tourist destination.

I've spent some time in Hampstead, once three full weeks, walking the few miles down the Finchley Road into central London, chatting with the engaging fellow who runs the little Italian inn on the high street and who makes an excellent cup of coffee, sipping beer with my daughter on the terrace of an ancient pub, and sitting on the bench in front of Keats House daydreaming and writing.

When you sit on the bench there on a sunny summer day, facing the becalmed street in front of you and surrounded by trees, flowers, and that special quiet that descends in leafy upscale urban neighborhoods, a quiet of serious money, whispering nannies, and hushed sprinklers, you enter (if you're not stewing about questions of privilege) a particular kind of space, the space of the creator's daydream.

It is a space in which whole novels appear, maybe great ones, maybe mediocre ones, but entirely vivid and fully realized ones. In this serene sanctuary your nattering monkey mind is sedated and there is nothing left for your brain to do but spin out creation. It is a space in which you get to imagine—just as you get to imagine wherever you happen to find yourself, of course, but more easily here in the dappled light and surrounded by skittering finches.

This is a spot where you can imagine your novel from beginning to end: if, that is, you will let the spot work its magic. The perfection of this place amounts to absolutely nothing if you prevent yourself from daydreaming creations into existence. If you have the bad habit of populating pregnant places with your commonest thoughts, if you can't make the switch from busy mind to silence, if you haven't cultivated the habit of creating-at-will in the world, then you won't last three minutes on this bench. Your hopping mind will hop you right up.

The typical tourist ensconced on this bench smiles at the natural beauty surrounding him. The writer is obliged to ignore and transcend that beauty. It is one thing if he is also a visual artist:

then it's proper for him to train his eye on this leafy paradise in a hunt for subject matter. But if he's a writer, then he mustn't be a flower cataloguer and a bird watcher. His job is to get lost in a timeless, weightless, sightless daydream that arises because his neurons have relaxed themselves in the modest warmth of a London summer day and, relaxed now, have gathered to make art.

It's a matter of good habits versus bad habits. It may be the case that you have cultivated the good habit of fruitfully daydreaming the second you hear the lap of waves, the singing of jays, or the click of your study door closing. Or you may have cultivated the bad habit of always distracting yourself from your art. That, sad to say, is what happens too often. Writers and would-be writers get in the bad habit, sometimes the lifelong bad habit, of filling every space, even the most sunlit and auspicious ones, with pennyweight, sandpapery thoughts designed to keep their imagination at bay.

Here is what you might do while sitting on Keats's bench if you are the victim of this bad habit:

- You could internally object to the price of admission to Keats House, which is about $7, and go on to complain not only about that travesty but about the price of everything in London, from tube rides to take-out food (fish-and-chips at $18? My god!).

153

- You could recite Keats's "Ode on a Grecian Urn" and "Ode to a Nightingale," written here during the period 1818–1820, and marvel at their lyricism, vigor, and so on, thus making sure to keep your head filled with other people's words.
- You could enter into conversation with a passing docent and learn in which room Keats wrote what, which tea he preferred, whether he wrote in the morning or at night, and thirty or forty other facts whose lack of importance can't be overestimated.
- You could remind yourself that you are a mere two blocks from Heath Street, where, when you strolled here, you passed a boutique body shop with luscious scents, a charming greengrocer's sporting perfect summer peaches and plums, and a closet-sized bookstore with impressive antique maps. You could be on Heath Street in two minutes flat. . . .
- You could tsk-tsk at the arriving schoolchildren who, yes, are making some noise; you could remind yourself that on your flight home you have a middle seat and will probably die from the constriction and boredom; you could plan your evening (drinks, dinner and a show?); you could worry about your lover, who, by choosing not to make this trip, probably announced a philandering intention; you could . . . well, you could keep your poor brain as busy as a beehive struck by a stick, if that is your unfortunate habit.

If you have this bad habit of constantly stifling your imagination, you might try the following.

1. Set aside some imagining time, maybe twenty minutes or even an hour.
2. Smile a little, by way of alerting yourself to the fact that you mean to get dreamy and visit faraway places.
3. Slowly silence your busy thoughts. Imagine that you have a knob, like the knob on a tuner, that you can turn to lower the sound. Lower the sound on your thoughts until they are extinguished.
4. Keep smiling, even though the ensuing silence is a little unnerving.
5. Wait, holding the heartfelt intention that you will keep the door to your imagination open for as long as it takes, until blue elephants, space settlements, or your new novel strolls right in.
6. Wait, smiling, as if the moment to open presents was rapidly approaching.
7. Keep waiting. The longer you wait, the stronger the muscle you'll build, the one you flex when you want to imagine.

Try this same tactic when you arrive at the bench in your town square, your neighborhood park, your outdoor mall, your own backyard, or your business complex. You can completely prevent yourself from fruitfully daydreaming by keeping yourself busy and distracted, or you can mindfully make an opening for your dreams and ideas to enter. What's your preference?

This opening to imagination doesn't happen automatically, anymore than do openings to other dimensions. You have to separate the folds of warped space in order to time-travel; you have to silence your everyday mind in order to imagine. Accept that you will need to practice. It is a funny kind of practice, practicing right silence and dreamy readiness, but a necessary one.

LESSON 24

You get to use your imagination only if you allow yourself to use your imagination. Like an omnipotent evil elf, you have the power to completely cut yourself off from your imagination. Enlist your good elf self, the part of you that wants to bring new worlds into existence.

To Do

1. Buy a garden bench. Put it anywhere, either indoors or outdoors. Practice the seven-step imagination routine outlined above.
2. Forget the garden bench. Get a folding chair. Let's get started!
3. Buy your imagination a present. What would it like?
4. Open your imagination.

CHAPTER 25

The Richly Imagined Paragraph

There are two ways (at least) to use the space that the opening paragraph of a piece of prose provides. One is to produce a paragraph that offers up no particular clues as to where you are going. The other is to produce a road map in a nutshell. In the first instance the reader "can't imagine" where this journey will take him and in the second instance not only can he, but he is primed to begin spinning out his own fascinating scenarios.

You can create a road map right in that first paragraph without, at the same time, providing a reader with too much—without, that is, killing off suspense or telegraphing your highlights. Each writing unit—the sentence, the paragraph, the page, the chapter—can hold your rich imaginings in a complete way: you don't have to reserve those riches for a big scene in the middle or for a plot twist near the end.

A paragraph is its own space to be decorated, maybe as small a space as that tiny guest bedroom in the back of your house but just as valuable. It deserves your full, wide-open imagination. It isn't just a marker, an empty shoe bin, another 120 words getting you from here to there. It is a world—or can be. It can do what the following first paragraphs do, taken from a hypothetical collection of essays linked by their London setting.

LOVING LONDON

"London is no more representative of England than Paris is representative of France or Manhattan is representative of the United States. When Lenin comes to England to study, he doesn't settle in the Cotswolds: he comes to London. When Freud flees from the Nazis, he doesn't settle in Newcastle: he comes to London. London is a world city and the world arrives, to study, to hide out, to write, to begin a new life. Of the total population of the United Kingdom's ethnic minorities, half live in London. It is that kind of place, a place that tugs at the heart not because it is quaint but because it is rich with humanity in all its diversity."

HIGH SCHOOL READING

"You probably first encountered England, that faraway land, in something you read in high school. Maybe it was *Pride and Preju-*

dice, *Wuthering Heights*, *Return of the Native*, *Oliver Twist*, or some Chaucer or Shakespeare. An England began to take shape in your mind, an England of conniving kings, country parsons, Cockney accents, and carriages rattling on cobblestones. Given that you grew up on storybook England, what are you going to make of the real thing? For this is twenty-first century London, with its wine bars and terrorist threats, and not some Dickensian postcard."

The Enormity of It All

"London is huge—or tiny, depending on which London you mean. The City of London is a mere ripple in the pond of Greater London, which is a mind-boggling 874 square miles in size, the equivalent of twenty San Franciscos and double the size of that other unholy-sized city, Los Angeles. One morning, all-day bus pass in hand, I embark on the grand tour of this monstrosity, London from Ealing (in the west) to West Ham (in the east), from Southgate (in the north) to Norbury (in the south), taking in the sights that do not interest tourists but that feed writers: the graffiti, the queues, the curving streets, the pub that looks just right to write in."

Bloomsbury Yesterday and Today

"In certain circles it is not unusual to find that Jane, although married to Joe, and even in some sense happily married, is also sleeping with Janet. Those circles are the urban ones, where the pieties of the culture-at-large get punctured with splendid regularity. You will find Janes of this sort in Berlin, in Paris, in Los Angeles . . . and of course in Bloomsbury, that London neighborhood and state of mind, where Virginia Woolf and Vita Sackville-West made love and legends."

Food From the Colonies

"I used to make Indian food from scratch, toasting the cumin seeds, whirring the onion paste, and occasionally simmering a vat of our all-time favorite, tomato chutney with slivered almonds and several whole heads (not cloves) of garlic. Then the children came; goodbye tomato chutney, hello take-out pizza. I am reminded of my savory days by London's scadillion Indian restaurants, its Bengal Lancer and Chutney Mary and Cinnamon Club, each of which raises the poignant question: what does a colonial history do to the colonized—and to the colonizer?"

Freud in London

"Freud, that man of ideas, was also a materialist, a sensualist, and something else, something to which his famous couch attests. That couch, residing in the London house to which Freud fled after the Nazi annexation of Austria, is covered with an Iranian rug, piled high with chenille cushions, and surrounded by Tabriz rugs. We are reminded of Sherlock Holmes, the aristocratic use of heroin and cocaine, and Freud's own addictions. So it is really not so surprising, looking around this room, to suddenly realize that Freud was an addict who created a treatment regimen designed, like a cigarette with additives, to addict the patient to his psychoanalyst."

If you'd like to create a road map right at the beginning of the piece you're intending to write, try the following. Quiet your mind, open up to possibility, and let an idea come forward, maybe in the form of a phrase: say, "Freud in London." Do not stop there but travel in your mind's eye along the length of your unwritten and hitherto unimagined piece, writing it, as it were, in thin air, writing the whole 1,500-word essay (if that's what it turns out to be) in five or ten seconds flat.

You'll find that you've returned from your imaginings with images, sentences, an arc, a sense of having traveled, and the way to create your opening paragraph. Write that paragraph. Give the piece a title—the title is right there, waiting for you. Then make the journey a second time and write the concluding paragraph. Haven't you just accomplished something very interesting?

You might repeat the process, keeping in the back of your mind the phrase "themed collection," and within the hour have the titles, opening paragraphs, and concluding paragraphs of several pieces for a collection—a collection that was available to you all along but that needed exactly this invitation.

LESSON 25

Use your powers of imagination so regularly and so naturally that every inch of your writing feels richly imagined, whether it's the first moody sentence or the heart-pounding conclusion.

To Do

1. Create a world in a sentence.
2. Create a world in a paragraph.
3. Create a world in a page.
4. Imagine a piece of writing from beginning to end and "come back" with its first paragraph, one that captures something rich about the journey you just took. Then title the piece. Then write its last paragraph. Then celebrate a little, perhaps by repeating the process or by completing the piece in one sitting.

Part VII

Public Space

CHAPTER 26

Saying Something

J've seen some good movies lately: the Australian movie *Somersault*, the Spanish movie *Nobody's Life*, the American movie *Winter Passing*, and the German movie *Head On*, by the Turkish-German director Fatih Akin. In each, the director chose "difficult material" to explore and was willing to say what was on his or her mind. They had opinions; they were not neutral; their first objective was not to sell at all costs. I am currently working with a well-known documentary filmmaker on her first feature film and we, too, are in this territory: the territory of trying to really say something.

Consider the following. It is a few years ago. One Saturday morning in Paris I step out from the apartment building where I am staying onto the rue Saint Gilles. Across the street is "something"—now, how shall I describe that something? I could say "on the other side of the street a father and his three children are approaching." How little that description would capture of what I feel to be true about those figures! If I wrote such a phrase and left the matter at that, it would only be because I wanted to keep vague what these people signify to me. I would be playing it safe. It would also bore you to tears. "On the other side of the street a father and his three children are approaching." How nothing! How nothing on purpose.

What if I was willing to add my real thoughts? I know, for instance, that this man is an Orthodox Jew and that he and his children are returning from temple. I know this because I grew up as a non-observant Jew in Brooklyn and because I know every nuance of what "going to temple" and what "coming home from temple" looks like. I know, for instance, that they are coming back from temple and not going, though I don't know how I know that. Is it because of the time of day, something in their look, something in their attitude? I couldn't tell you—but I know.

What about the important person who is not there—his wife and their mother? I could leave her out of my description and hope that you noticed her absence—but would you notice? I certainly want you to notice. I want to make sure that you don't miss the fact that she is absent, since I want to provoke you into thinking what her absence might mean. Of course, it might mean anything. She and her husband might be divorced. She might be shopping. She might be preparing lunch. But it also might mean—and this is the thought I want you to entertain—that she isn't all that welcome at temple.

Then there is the matter of how they are approaching. They are hurrying, and "hurrying" is its own kind of loaded word. Children sometimes hurry to school or to catch a bus but their natural way is not to hurry. They only hurry when they feel compelled to hurry. Therefore to say that they are hurrying after their father is to suggest that they are under some compulsion. I would hope that by my identifying their passage as "hurrying," you sense that their Sabbath is not a joy but marching orders. That's what I'd like you to get if I describe them as hurrying.

I can leave things out; I can put things in; but in every instance I am saying something. Once you realize that there is no such thing as innocent describing, you will begin to feel liberated. There may be real trees in nature but there are no real trees appearing in artists' drawings, paintings, sculptures, or photographs. An artist can photograph a forest when a cloud is passing and make it sinister. He can wait for the cloud to blow by and present us with a happy little forest. The very attempt at artistic neutrality is itself a blatant position. Try describing the bombing of Hiroshima as an interesting example of atomic physics and see if you aren't making a statement! There is no artistic neutrality—forget about it.

I am suggesting that you make bolder, more honest choices. There is no such thing as neutrality: say what you intend to say.

If you wanted to write a history of Paris, for instance, would you feel compelled to start at the beginning? That is no more the truth of the matter than starting yesterday. All historical records are subjective, pointed constructions. Ninety-nine percent must be left out and whatever is left in is not the truth but a point of view. The question is not "What is the real history of Paris?" but rather "What is your intention?"

You could start with the Parisii, those Celtic folk, settling by the Seine on the Ile de la Cité in 300 B.C. and starting a little fishing village; or with Caesar invading Gaul in 52 B.C., renaming the fishing village Lutetia, and watching it overflow onto the Left Bank; or with King Clovis and his Frankish followers, who defeat the Romans in 486 and rename Lutetia Paris; or with Charlemagne; or with the Black Death; or with the Hundred Years' War. Is any one of these the "true" starting place?

What about its intellectual history? The University of Paris is established in 1215 and the Sorbonne in 1253 but it takes another 500 years before we see the movement to establish the supremacy of the individual known as the Enlightenment. Claude Helvétius writes the free-thinking *Essays on the Mind*, it is condemned as godless by the Pope and the Parlement of Paris and publicly burned, and it becomes the most widely read book of its time. Diderot continues the project of compiling a comprehensive alphabetical treatment of human knowledge, the encyclopedia. Which part of this is the truth about Paris?

Fast-forward 200 years to the Paris of the structuralists and the postmodernists. Wielding the sharp sword of deconstruction, they make projects such as those of Diderot and the Encyclopedists seem ridiculous. In a mere two centuries we have moved from "the possibility of knowing everything" to "the impossibility of knowing anything." That is a fascinating historical thread—but no more true or false than the thread of Parisian massacres highlighted, for instance, by St. Bartholomew's Day, 1572, when Catherine de Médicis ordered 3,000 Protestants executed.

Writing is interpretation. You are obliged to offer yours. If you want to say nothing, offend no one, tell a happy little tale, and otherwise act the innocent, that choice is available to you. Just remember that even then you are saying something and that we are watching.

LESSON 26

You can play it safe or you can speak your mind. Why venture into the public space of readers and audiences if your goal is to keep your real thoughts private? If you are bothering to write, say what you mean.

To Do

1. Make a list of the issues you are willing to shed some blood over. Read your list over. Are you writing about any of these? If not, why not?
2. Get a soapbox and set it up in the middle of your living room. See what it feels like to stand on a soapbox and say what's on your mind. Does it feel dangerous? Do you feel ridiculous? Acknowledge your feelings but do not stop speaking.
3. Put that soapbox in a public place. Do that literally; or do it by saying something in writing.
4. Say what you mean. The long silence will come soon enough.

CHAPTER 27

Standing Up

A ngelina Grimké, the daughter of an aristocratic, slave-holding Southern family, became, as a matter of conscience, an abolitionist. Publicly championing the unpopular abolitionist cause constituted an act of engagement and an example of conscience in action. In 1835, Angelina converted her older sister Sarah to the abolitionist cause and together they became the first women to speak in public for the black slave and, later, for women's rights. They became founding activists in a pair of vital movements.

As activists, they persuaded their mother to give them the slaves who constituted their share of the family estate, whom they immediately freed. In part as a testament to their Quaker faith, they began speaking and lecturing in New York and New England against slavery, speaking engagements that included

Angelina's three effective appearances before the Massachusetts legislative committee on antislavery petitions in 1838.

In addition, Sarah wrote, among other nonfiction pieces, *An Epistle to the Clergy of the Southern States* (1836), urging abolition, and *Letters on the Equality of the Sexes and the Condition of Woman* (1837). Angelina wrote *An Appeal to the Christian Women of the South* (1836). Standing up for abolition equaled engagement; speaking out made them activists; but quietly sitting and dealing with the challenges that attend to writing an effective nonfiction piece amounted to something else. Creating something that could move a listener constituted an act of engaged creativity. This is a primary way that a writer can stand up for what she believes, by filling public spaces with her creative efforts.

A songwriter, when he attends a rally, is engaged. If he helps organize the rally, he is an activist. But when he composes a song for the cause, that composing is an act of engaged creativity. It is an act that requires that he make use of his talents, skills, mind, heart, hands, and personal presence in ways that are different from—not better than or more courageous than, but different from—the way he uses himself when he signs a petition, writes a check, or builds a barricade. In exactly the same sense, a physician who travels to Africa without pay to provide medical services for the indigent poor is engaged and an activist; but if, upon arriving, she discovers that she must invent new procedures because of conditions on the ground, that need demands that she engage the creative part of her nature, the part that innovates and dreams up new combinations. Both the protest song and the new procedure are acts of engaged creativity, that is, creative effort in ethical service.

Engagement is conscience in action and engaged creativity is creative effort in ethical service. A writer can do his part in the struggle to keep civilization afloat in two different ways: as a person and in his art. As a person, there are organizations to join and movements to support. He can also turn over a portion of his time to making art with an overt social and political bent, as, for instance, Richard Dawkins did when he wrote *The God Delusion* or Michael Isikoff and David Corn did when they wrote *Hubris: The Inside Story of Spin, Scandal and the Selling of Iraq*. That is a real option.

"Engagement" is not a new word or a new idea and "the engaged artist" is a well-known designation in existential literature. Both "engaged creativity" and "the engaged artist" are useful phrases and we should begin to use them—and live them—more. An "engaged artist" is someone whose body of work is political and who perhaps is always political. This is admirable but it may not be the way you want to live your life. "Engaged creativity," by contrast, only requires that you spend a percentage of your time on sociopolitical writing. Maybe you write one kind of novel most of the time but every so often you try your hand at a *Brave New World* or an *Animal Farm*.

We need our writers to bring their best efforts to the struggle against the reactionary forces that, wherever and whenever they can, tyrannize others. We need our writers to create iconic work that speaks the truth and that provides us with a powerful shorthand way of thinking and speaking—a shorthand such as "Kafkaesque" and "Orwellian." We need these things more every day. Most writers do not want to do this work as their only work or as their primary work, but perhaps they can commit to being engaged part-time. Can you?

The domestic and worldwide forces lined up against reason and justice are considerably more powerful, more ruthless, and more single-minded than we are. They have slogans and enforcers: we seem always to have only ourselves. Because we seem only to have ourselves, we feel exhausted and defeated even before we begin. How can I, a lone individual, make a dent? We feel past absurdity, past irony, past despair, and find ourselves disempowered and equal only to watching television. And yet it is exactly where we find ourselves that we must make our significance.

I invite you onto the path of at least occasional "engaged creativity." There is a public space for you to inhabit as a writer, one where you add your voice to the voices of others and defend with your pen those principles you deem important. We need you there, in that public space, despite the risks to your livelihood, your friendships, and your place in society that you invite by going public.

LESSON 27

Pepper public spaces with some engaged writing in which you stand up for what you believe. You can still be charming; you can still be amusing; you can still be witty. Just be sure to stand up.

To Do

1. Take a risk in your writing, any kind of risk, so as to begin to acquire the habit of risk-taking as a writer. Remember that when you take a risk it is likely to feel risky! Learn to deal with the anxiety and fear that standing up provokes.
2. Pick an issue—illiteracy, intolerance, exploitation, the proliferation of nuclear weapons—and create a piece of fiction or nonfiction that is at once beautiful and polemical. Try your hand at marrying art and conviction.
3. Think about how you are holding the words "private" and "public." Are you intending to remain private even after your work goes public? Or are you ready to inhabit public spaces such as radio studios and lecture platforms?
4. Stand up. We need you.

CHAPTER 28

On Not Being Quite So Nice

It isn't so easy to write what's on our mind and let people in on our thoughts. We fear reprisals; we fear looking bad; we fear having to defend what we've said. It isn't so easy to write what's on our mind even if we are just writing in our journal: there is much that we are keeping hidden from ourselves and our natural frankness is defeated by our defensiveness. The result of this self-censorship is that what we write is milder, more indirect, and less authentic than it would be if we had internal and external permission to speak.

John, a nonfiction writer, explained: "I've learned to be conciliatory rather than confrontational. It's a pretty good skill set that has served me well, but it has also limited me. I have always been a welcome member on any committee or board because, as one person once said, 'It is nice to have sanity represented.' I have often been the steadfast presence in the midst of political strife during my university career, helping to provide a container and sense of safety for others to be strident. I do not, however, like the word 'nice.' I think it stands for No Inner Core Evident. I do not think I am nice, nor do I want to be."

John's distinction is a useful one: you can be steadfast, conciliatory, compassionate, sensible, sane, and all the rest; at the same time you can have convictions, stand up for principles, reveal your warts, and express your moral outrage. The main thing is that you obtain internal permission to speak and do not fear "going public" with your innermost thoughts. Once you've obtained that permission, you can maintain mindful self-monitoring and decide what you want to reveal and when you want to reveal it.

Marcia, a poet, explained: "I know all about being nice. It would be so easy for me to remain invisible and write nice poems and read them to nice people at nice poetry readings. That is the norm. Earlier this year a friend of mine wrote a beautiful, passionate poem expressing her outrage about the Iraq war. Before she read this poem at a peace day event, she showed it to the event organizers and to her writing group, who collectively edited every ounce of passion out of it (we wouldn't want to offend the donors now, would we, or anybody else, for that matter). Compared to the original version, the poem she read at the event was dead."

We all experience internal and external pressure to "let the difficult stuff go." For instance, no one in my family wanted me to pursue a novel I was writing about moving Israel. The book's premise was that Israel, in order to survive, needed to be moved lock, stock, and bagel to a safer location, and the book's hero attempts that quixotic feat. The villains were Jews, Christians, Muslims, capitalists, patriots. . . . I aimed to excoriate everyone. In fact, I wrote the novel, but I made sure, by my terseness and indifferent handling of plot, that it could never be published. Just as happy as my family to see it rejected, I put it safely away in the storage shed.

We do not want to let fear stop us from writing what needs to be written and we don't want to write an ostensibly brave thing in such a way that we guarantee that it is not publishable. Nor do we want to blithely make all of our warts public.

Commenting on this last, Rachel, a novelist, explained, "I'm troubled by the relentless me-me-me-ism of much current writing. We seem to have an obsession with being able to say absolutely anything that's on our minds, no matter how hurtful it may be to others. I recall a nicely written, tragic autobiography about a woman who was badly treated as a child by her adoptive mother. The writing was electrifying and the story caused my jaw to drop, but I felt uncomfortable and like a voyeur for reading it."

What a balancing act we are obliged to manage, balancing our need to speak with issues of privacy, decency, and the rights of others! How much should we tell about our family, our neighbors, or our bosses? How many of our own warts should we reveal, and to what purpose? In *The Creativity Book*, for instance, I wanted to make the point that unless we're willing to reveal ourselves we probably won't do our deepest writing. I chose to reveal that I'd had a period during my Army days when I shoplifted clothes from the PX and gave the loot away to my fellow grunts. It was a fascinating process trying to decide what to reveal: I discovered that I could reveal only what I could reveal and not a single blemish more.

Often we fail to say what's on our mind because we fear that we won't be able to control ourselves once we create an opening for the truth to escape. A fear of "saying too much" and "going too far" is a significant part of why we censor ourselves. Then the question becomes, is the fear justified? Shouldn't we try as an exercise to say some of the things that we're feeling, to see if we actually lose control or, just as likely, modulate and moderate our revelations just perfectly? I propose that exercise to you right now. Write about something that you've previously censored out of your writing.

LESSON 28

We all censor ourselves. Think carefully about whether you want to draw a different line in the sand and reveal more of your truth in your writing.

To Do

1. Sit down to write your current piece or your next piece. As you begin, try to notice whether a part of you is already beginning to censor your efforts. Does your censor occupy a certain "space" in your psyche? What if you opened the back door of your psychic space and shooed him or her out. Does that seem possible?

2. Instead of shooing your censor out the door, try the following trick. Send him or her out for soft drinks and potato chips. As soon as your censor leaves, start writing!

3. Decide that when you sit down at your writing desk, you will speak with passion and power and let the chips fall where they may.

4. Keep making the effort to tell your truth.

CHAPTER 29

Two Weeks in Italy

Jn the first section on physical space we chatted about adding public spaces to your primary writing space: adding a café, a park bench in the sun, your train ride into the city each morning, your train ride home. Some of these places, such as your local café, you visit on purpose so as to write. In others, you simply find yourself there, and to get your writing done you have to do it right there. When you write in either place, you honor your pledge not to let self-consciousness prevent you from writing.

Let's continue this theme. In what is so far a series of two volumes, *A Writer's Paris* and *A Writer's San Francisco*, I argued that certain places have a special resonance for writers and that a writing life ought to include those places at least occasionally. You must write where you are, as that is where you are; and wishing you were elsewhere will not help your current novel. But if you can also get away now and then to a place that warms your heart, sparks your mind, and satisfies your longing to travel, you'll have satisfied a dream and set the stage for some excellent on-the-road writing.

Maybe you're hoping to spend some time in Greenwich Village, Paris, London, Rome, Barcelona, Berlin, or Tokyo. Maybe it's Provence, Tuscany, Brittany, the Cotswolds, or the Scottish Highlands. If a place has associations for you, if it excites you to imagine traveling there and writing there, that's the sort of place I have in mind. Yours may be a traditional choice such as Paris or an idiosyncratic one such as Lyon or Strasbourg. Maybe it's Seattle, Singapore, or the South Side of Chicago. Maybe it's a place whose name nobody would recognize, a Texas hill town, an out-of-the-way Louisiana parish. It might be a place with an international airport or a place that can only be reached by a local bus. If it has meaning for you, if something in you is stirred by imagining yourself there, sitting, staring, walking, and writing, that is a place you owe yourself a writing visit.

The main preparations you need to make, in addition to rounding up the money and making your travel arrangements, are internal. You want to go as a writer, not as a vacationer. You could go, soak up the atmosphere, not write anything except journal entries, and have a splendid time; but I'm suggesting something different.

I suggest that you actually write when you get there. Sitting in a Paris café with your laptop open and your novel humming is a special way to assert that you are writer, that you are taking your writing seriously, and that you are comfortable writing in public. For this to happen, you need to prepare yourself in the following way: by calling it a writing retreat, not a vacation; by bringing your writing tools and your current project; and by thinking as much about your writing as about your destination.

Your specialty is your own creative spirit; you don't need to immerse yourself in the history of the place you are visiting. Your stocks-in-trade are yearnings, not train schedules. You may speak nothing but English and fumble your way around strange towns. You may order everything—a room, a sandwich, a newspaper—only with great difficulty. Fine; so be it. Why prepare by filling your head with "Which way to the toilet?" and "Do those snails come with a salad?" when you could be encouraging the unfolding of your novel?

You may not know what you're doing when it's time to order or to hop off a train. But you know exactly what you're doing when you sit on a bench in a small square in Paris or in a tiny Spanish hamlet. You're meditating on what surrounds you— a boy and a girl in uniform waiting for the school bus, cars half the size of the cars at home angling into parking spots into which they can't possibly fit—feeling the sun on your forehead,

185

participating in the human experiment in that special way of a traveling writer, and, after a while, opening your pad and writing.

It is that human experiment that you are writing about, the one that produced Moorish architecture, Irish bagpipes, the paintings of Goya, tulips in every conceivable color, strife, complex ideas, simple folk dances, and cobblestone streets that engage your imagination while they hurt your feet. If you weren't alive to the amazing experiment of which we are each a part, you would travel only for business or to visit relatives. Something inside of you needs to compare one blue sky against another, to walk in the footsteps of itinerant monks and expressionist painters, and to take the measure of our species in small bars where you understand little except the warmth of the bodies around you. That's why you're on the road: because the writer in you demands it.

Travel as the writer you are. Planning for a trip is only in part about purchasing tickets and packing light. It is more importantly about opening to your creative nature, readying yourself to be receptive to what you're about to experience, and selecting an itinerary that serves your imagination, your beauty receptors, and your spirit. It's saying to yourself, loudly and clearly, "During these two weeks in Italy I am going to outline my Italian novel and come back with a ton of scenes, so many scenes that it won't even bother me that I put on three pounds from all that gelato."

The trip begins. You actually bring your laptop, even though that doesn't feel so festive, and you turn it on as soon as you pass through the security checkpoint at the airport. For that long hour before it's time to board, you write. No one else is writing; you are already proving the exception. The writer across from you is reading a mystery, the writer down the row is checking her e-mail; you are writing. You board; you take off; you gain altitude; it's announced that the use of electronic devices is now permitted. The other writers on the plane do not accept this offer; you pull out your laptop and resume writing.

If this doesn't sound like a traditional vacation, where you leave your work at home, well, it isn't. It's a busman's holiday. A rock climber arrives in the Alps ready to climb. A scuba diver arrives in Aruba ready to dive. You arrive in Budapest raring to write. You skip the museums and the monuments and rush headlong to some grand nineteenth-century café where chess players still gather; you order your Viennese pastry and your espresso; and you begin your lavish busman's holiday by pulling out your laptop. Let the tourists take stock of the monuments; you have scribbling to do.

Lesson 29

Take the occasional writing retreat, making Paris, London, some Hawaiian black beach, a cabin in Maine, or that bed-and-breakfast across town your writing space for a glorious busman's week.

To Do

1. Set yourself the task of writing in public. Then do it. This is a good thing in and of itself and also crucial preparation for your writing holiday.
2. Once you've mastered writing in public, plan your writing retreat.
3. Take it.
4. Enjoy it!—and remember to write!

Part VIII

Existential Space

CHAPTER 30

The Way of the Meaning-Maker

When our youngest daughter came home from college at Thanksgiving one year she gave me a coffee mug as a present. The motto on the coffee mug read: "Life isn't about finding yourself. Life is about creating yourself." "Isn't that your philosophy in a nutshell?" she laughed. She was exactly right. "Anonymous" had captured the essence of two centuries of existential thought: that life is as much a responsibility as a gift and that each of us is honor bound to create ourselves in our own best image.

I make my meaning; none exists until I make it. All that exists until I make personal meaning is the possibility of meaning. There is the possibility that I will experience the next hour as meaningful. There is the possibility that I will experience my relationship with my mate and children as meaningful. There is the possibility that I will experience my life as meaningful. If I do not make the meaning that is waiting to be made, I'll have squandered the opportunity to live life on my own terms.

It doesn't matter that you have a sanctified study, a fast computer, a great idea, a splendid way with commas, or any other writer's tool or habit, if you don't also adopt the mantle of meaning-maker and announce, especially to yourself, that you must create the meaning in your life. Unless you inhabit existential space in precisely this fashion, as a meaning-maker the chances are great that you'll opt for a respectful silence as you wait for meaning to drop into your lap.

To stand up as a meaning-maker is a revolutionary stance. The groundwork for this revolution has been laid by 200 years of movement toward a single idea: that life can have meaning even if the universe has none. While each of us is limited by circumstances and by our appetites, defenses, and other frailties and realities, we are nevertheless free to choose what meaning we intend to make. This nature has granted us. I get to decide what will make me feel righteous and happy and so do you. Your life has meaning only when you invest it with meaning.

You are the sole arbiter of the meaning. The second you turn to someone else and ask "What does life mean?" you've slipped into a way of thinking that courts inauthenticity and depression. The second you agree with someone simply because of his position or reputation, whether that someone is a guru, author, cleric, parent, politician, general, elder, editor, or literary agent, you fall from the path of personal meaning-making and become flimsy and ordinary.

You and you alone get to decide about meaning. That is the awesome proposition facing every contemporary person. As limited as we are in a biological and psychological sense, we are exactly that free in an existential sense. If we do not live that way, honoring that existential freedom, we get nightmares and panic attacks. If we do not live that way, we find ourselves wishing that we had opted for authenticity and decided to matter. If we do not live that way, we wish we had.

Maybe it is painful for you to think that you are a disposable throwaway in a meaningless universe and that there is nothing you can possibly do to alter that reality. Let that pain go right this instant and announce that meaning can still exist, just as soon as you make some. The split second you do this, all previous belief systems—those that told you what to believe and those that told you there was nothing to believe—vanish. You get to let go of wondering what the universe wants of you and the fear that nothing matters as you proudly announce that you will make life mean exactly what you intend it to mean. What a triumphant announcement!

To be sure, after that triumphant announcement there you are, exactly where you were the moment before. Has anything changed? Yes, something vital. The instant you realize that meaning is not provided (as traditional belief systems teach) and that it is not absent (as nihilists feel), a new world of potential opens up for you. You suddenly have the philosophical and psychological pillars to support your new meaning-making efforts. You break free of tradition, with its restrictions, demands, and narcissistic bent and set out to make your life a thing of value. You haven't made it that thing yet, simply by announcing your intention. But you've aimed yourself in a brilliant direction: in the direction of your own creation.

This path may not sound all that radical, but it is. It is a radical departure from the traditional path because it blasts all received knowing out of the water. Its central tenet, that you must decide for yourself, is exactly the following announcement: you create your universe from your best understanding of what is right, what is good, and what is valuable. Nothing and no one is allowed to prevent you from deciding what values you intend to uphold and how your righteousness and heroism will play itself out.

It is an equally radical departure from the forlorn postmodern position, which moves from what is likely a fact, that we are throwaway creatures deluded about our own importance, to the unwarranted conclusion that life is not worth taking seriously. The conclusion is unwarranted because it takes a certain thought and a certain feeling, that we do not matter and that despair must follow, and elevates them above an equally available thought, that life can be lived seriously, and an equally available feeling, that of full engagement. You trump nihilism with the amazing announcement that meaning is exactly as available as meaninglessness.

The way of the meaning-maker is a path to make a person proud. You heroically step out into the blinding light of reality, look around, and say, "I am going to do this and I am going to do it for these reasons." You make the next hour meaningful by investing it with your capital, your intentions, your energy, and your decisiveness. You make the hour after that meaningful in exactly the same way. You do this hour in and hour out, year after year, sometimes sitting and staring, sometimes hugging and kissing, sometimes working ferociously, always for reasons that you deem important. You aren't a god—you are too earthbound for that. But you are the best human being you can make yourself, the one you had always hoped to see in the mirror.

That is the writer's existential position, her existential space, her existential shout. She makes the calculation that her best bet is to act as if her life matters and her writing matters, and she seals the deal by actually writing. At the end of the day she is repaid by the feeling that she gave life a bloody good shot.

LESSON 30

Waiting for meaning is a mistake. Seeking meaning is a mistake. Accepting meaning is a mistake. Bemoaning the absence of meaning is a mistake. The only authentic path is to make meaning. You stand up, gather your wits, and exclaim, "I have decided!" Then you clap yourself on the back and get started.

To Do

1. Bring forward a writing project that best resembles "an investment of meaning" and launch into it.
2. Design a "way of the meaning-maker" crest and sew it into all of your clothes. Or, less fancifully, make an effort to educate yourself about which of your projects hold the most meaning for you. Annotate your to-do list of upcoming writing projects with your thoughts about the meaningfulness of each project on the list.
3. Picture the next hour "devoid of meaning" and then picture it "brimming over with meaning." What did you just learn?
4. Look back (in your mind's eye) at the writing you've done over the past year or two. Can you discern which pieces felt more meaningful and which felt less meaningful? Do the more meaningful pieces share anything in common?

CHAPTER 31

Embracing Tremors

J t's easy to throw up your hands and cry, "I don't get this idea of meaning-making. How can you make meaning? Either there is meaning or there isn't. You can't just make meaning like you can make a convertible or a violin. No, I don't get it—so I think I'll pass!" This objection is at once reasonable and fully disingenuous. It is disingenuous because each of us knows in our bones exactly what the phrase "making meaning" signifies. We know perfectly well that it is composed of ideas such as personal responsibility, courage, engagement, and authenticity. There isn't a thing unclear about it.

However, part of the objection is reasonable—the part where we cry out in pain. What we are objecting to is not the obscurity of the phrase but the nature of the universe the phrase posits. We object to a universe where meaning has to be made. We object to a universe that is meaningless until we force it to mean. We object to nature pulling this dirty trick and making us a partner to it, giving us exactly two choices, to not look this reality square in the eye and live as a coward, or to see what is required and live as an absurd hero. It is not the obscurity of the phrase "making meaning" that disturbs us but what it says about life.

How do we meet the objection that we would like life to be something other than what it is? We meet it with maturity and equanimity. We gracefully accept that meaning must be made, that meaning can be lost in the blink of an eye, that meanings change, and so on. We just stand up—which is exactly what we know we want to do.

Naturally this standing up, though an act of bravery, produces new anxieties. It is like a person in an occupied country bravely deciding to become a partisan—and then realizing what that entails. Isn't one of our genetic goals to reduce our experience of anxiety? Yes, but that isn't a goal of our humanity. Our genes tell us to avoid dark tunnels; our humanity tells us to explore them if that's where we'll find our writing. Your choice to avoid anxiety at all costs or to embrace the anxiety that comes with living authentically determines how you will live your life. If you decide that reducing your experience of anxiety is your paramount goal, you will never be a partisan.

We lose our taste for roller coasters when we get older. At fourteen, we can't wait to get on the Wild Monkey or the Ultimate Plunge. At forty, we can wait. Likewise, our taste for anxiety does not increase. We mind our grandchildren with an even more watchful eye than we minded our children, we move our money to safer investments, and we take fewer risks and invite fewer heart palpitations. This is the natural way. Still, in order to live authentically, we must risk anxiety, brave anxiety, embrace anxiety, and invite anxiety every single day. For a meaning-maker, there is no retirement from anxiety.

So make this choice—even though choosing itself provokes anxiety. Meaning-making requires that you make one mindful choice after another. There is no intellectual freedom, no personal freedom, no human freedom without a commitment to lifelong choosing. When a value that means something to you is involved, you must make a choice or fail yourself by not choosing. When work that means something to you is at stake, you must choose to do it or fail yourself by not choosing to do it. You must choose to choose: a day without mindful choosing is a day without meaning.

You must choose even though choosing settles nothing. Our meanings are bound to change as we decide to invest meaning here, remove meaning there, and monitor our meaning investments. New choices—including contradicting yourself from one day to the next—will prove necessary. How unsettling to be for a war on Monday and against it on Tuesday, as our understanding of the situation changes; these are among our worst feelings, having our world turned upside down overnight. Still, we must bravely change our minds and our meanings and make the choices that fit today, not yesterday.

You can manage to live a settled life, existentially speaking, and reduce the number of choices you need to make by adopting overarching positions such as "my country is always right" or "I only write for money." But you can only accomplish this anxiety reduction at the cost of your integrity. It is much better, although more nerve-wracking, to accept that meaning will never be settled, that meaning is always at risk, and that meaning is a challenge and not a foregone conclusion. Agreeing to this is like agreeing to live on an active fault line. There is no reason why you should agree with a smile and no reason why you should feel sanguine about surviving. But what you lose in safety you gain in authenticity.

LESSON 31

Existential space is shifting space. Make appropriate meaning today; tomorrow make the meaning appropriate for tomorrow.

To Do

1. Have a rousing debate with yourself about whether meaning ought to stay put or whether it is appropriate for it to (uncomfortably and even unaccountably) shift. Describe a time when meaning shifted in your life. What caused the shift? How did it feel to have it shift? What were the consequences of that meaning sea change?
2. Look into the future. Can you see an important meaning that is likely to shift one day—maybe your work identity when you retire or your conception of yourself as a daily nurturer when your children leave the nest? How might you prepare yourself for such meaning shifts? Can they be prepared for beforehand?
3. Shift a meaning. See how sickening that feels. Then recover quickly.
4. Explain to yourself why you'd choose to live in a place where earthquakes, hurricanes, blizzards, or tornadoes are guaranteed.

CHAPTER 32

Using Your Existential Intelligence

For the past hundred years, since the advent of intelligence tests and intelligence testing, people were thought of—and thought of themselves—as falling somewhere along a continuum of intelligence that ran from incredibly high to above-average to average to below-average. It was never very clear "how much" intelligence any of these stops along the continuum represented, so it was impossible to say whether a person of average intelligence, for instance, had "enough" intelligence for a particular task, whether that task was learning theoretical physics or voting in an election. It was simply taken for granted that average intelligence—the intelligence manifested by most people—was "good enough" to handle the ordinary tasks of living.

It was presumed that ordinary intelligence was "intelligence enough" to work in the world, abide by society's laws, and be able to understand everything from contracts to the math lessons encountered in school. Certainly it was easy enough to believe that a person who needed five tries at the bar exam was not quite as sharp as a person who aced it on the first try and that a great checkers player was not quite the intellectual equal of a chess grandmaster. But distinctions of this sort remained entirely impressionistic, arbitrary, and whimsical. Little was known or could be said about intelligence because the concept was murky at best.

Since "intelligence" remained so murky a concept, the integrity, utility, and meaningfulness of intelligence tests were easy to dispute, as was the idea of "unitary intelligence." Naturally enough, the idea of "multiple intelligences" arose. From this new point of view, people were no longer smart or not smart but rather smart or not smart in particular ways, a genius here and an idiot there, competent with respect to this and incompetent with respect to that.

Howard Gardner, the leading proponent of multiple intelligence theory, named first seven intelligences and then an eighth intelligence: linguistic intelligence ("word smart, as in a poet"); logical-mathematical intelligence ("number/reasoning smart, as in a scientist"); spatial intelligence ("picture smart, as in a sculptor or airplane pilot"); bodily-kinesthetic intelligence ("body smart, as in an athlete or dancer"); musical intelligence ("music smart, as in a composer"); interpersonal intelligence ("people smart, as in a salesman or teacher"); intrapersonal intelligence ("self smart, exhibited by individuals with accurate views of themselves"); and, later, naturalist intelligence ("nature smart, as in a naturalist").

At the end of the day, and even after the introduction of additional intelligences like Daniel Goleman's "emotional intelligence," we were still left with a large hole in the middle of the intelligence debate. First, none of these constructs got at our felt sense of what it meant to say that someone was or wasn't smart. Second, after a moment's thought you began to realize how many disparate ideas were being squashed together into one construct: natural differences, cultural differences, experiential differences, attitudinal differences, motivational differences, and so on. Third, and most important, the theory failed to address the following vital question: which intelligence or aspect of intelligence allowed you to comprehend what anything meant?

It turned out that the intelligence pundits had failed, until Gardner's recent introduction of a ninth intelligence, to describe or even consider our most important intelligence: our existential intelligence. Existential intelligence is the part of our nature that steps back, slips on a wide-angle lens, and appraises in the realm of meaning. It is our most important intelligence because it allows us to know what to do with the other intelligences.

We may have a great gift for visual representation; but it is our existential intelligence that allows us to know whether painting is the way we should spend our life. We may be capable in any number of ways, but we are just a bundle of capabilities until we apply our existential intelligence. Existential intelligence is the intelligence, the coordinating intelligence, the intelligence that all the other intelligences serve.

In order to provide ourselves with intelligent answers to questions such as whether it is more meaningful to write this novel, set in a desolate future, or that novel, set in a hopeful present, we are obliged to turn to our existential intelligence. We can't answer such questions through the application of science, even if we are an Einstein; nor with music, even if we are a Beethoven; nor with words, even if we are a Shakespeare. We can only answer them through the application of existential intelligence: by applying our gift for meaning comprehension and meaning management.

Existential intelligence is the capacity for conceptualizing large questions about human existence, about the meaning of life, why we are born, why we die, what consciousness is, and how we got here. It is all that but it is much more. It is the intelligence we use to appraise the meaning of our life minute by minute. It is only existential intelligence that permits us to think through whether or not we should fight in a war or protest that war, renew our efforts to live or take our life, embrace our culture or rebel against it, manifest our compassion or manifest our rage. Anything that we intend to do thoughtfully requires the application of our existential intelligence.

This is the intelligence that concerns you, as a writer, the most. It guides your writing themes, your writing choices, and your writing relationships. It helps you understand why you are bothering to write, why you are spending years on a recalcitrant book, why you are revising eight times when you would rather go fishing. The other intelligences are all well and good; your existential intelligence is key.

LESSON 32

Existential space is the space you inhabit when you want to consciously make decisions in the realm of meaning. You go there to shine the light of your existential intelligence on questions such as "What should I write?" and "How should I live?" Go there!

To Do

1. Test your existential intelligence by posing it a question such as "Which of these two potential projects is the more meaningful one?" See how it responds. Give it a letter grade and if it gets a poor grade, ask it to do better.

2. Test your friends by asking them questions in the realm of meaning, such as "What should a person do when a meaning crisis strikes?" or "How do you plug up a meaning leak when you feel the meaning draining out of your current writing project?" Rank-order your friends according to their answers. Then visit with the highest ranked among them for some meaningful conversations.
3. Raise your existential intelligence by making it feel welcome.
4. Raise it even further by using it.

Part IX

Epilogue
Creative Space: A Writing Fable

CHAPTER 33

Phoebe Chooses

Whit thirteen-year-old Phoebe got home from
school she found herself wondering whether she
should write a short story or perhaps begin a novel.
A story had the virtue of being short, pithy, and perhaps doable
before dinner (which today was tuna fish sandwiches and potato
salad, the kind of dinner you could be late for should your story
take all afternoon to write). A novel, which would take months
to write and could not possibly be finished before dinner, had the
virtue of allowing your characters to have the kinds of adventures that could only be found in, well, novels. This matter was
taxing Phoebe and she sat by the window in her room thinking
and thinking.

Harold Spider crawled by along the window ledge.

"Harold," Phoebe said. "I was wondering. I am in a writing
mood and I thought I might write a story about laundry drying

out-of-doors on a clothesline stretched between two trees. It would be a very atmospheric story full of starch smells and the inner lives of shirts and jeans. But I was also thinking that I might work on my novel set in the South Seas, having to do with an all-girl band stranded on a remote and scary island. The girls all have to play acoustic guitar, as there is no electricity! Isn't that clever? What do you think?"

"About?" Harold replied.

"Harold!" Phoebe scolded. "I just told you. Should I write the story or begin my novel?"

Harold scratched his head with several different legs. "I confess I am in a confused state of mind today. Why couldn't you do both? Or am I missing something important?"

Phoebe thought for a moment. Finally she nodded. "I suppose that's a reasonable question. On the face of it there's no reason not to do both. Yet there feels like there must be a reason. Wouldn't a muse know?"

Harold scratched his head again. "It's amazing how much we muses forget! Just last week someone I was visiting complained of exactly this problem—though that was about writing two songs, but it's the same thing really—and I know we arrived at the reason why she had to choose one or the other. But I can't remember what we concluded. She was twenty-three, by the way."

"How is that relevant?" Phoebe wondered skeptically.

"Well, I suppose I meant to imply that people of all ages find this to be a problem."

"Not just little girls like me?" Phoebe complained, trying to sound insulted. But actually she was pleased that her problem was a real, grown-up problem.

"I only meant—"

"Oh, pish-tosh!" Phoebe exclaimed. "Not to worry! But isn't this interesting and perplexing? I could write the short story today and then start the novel tomorrow. Why not? But I'm CONVINCED that I must choose one or the other and put the other one away, say in my little trunk over there, and if I don't I won't be able to get my whole head around either the laundry or the all-girl band."

"Maybe—"

"Wait! I'm thinking." She put her elbows on the sill and got into her very best thinking position, with her eyes shut.

Harold crawled away, to stretch his legs but also because it was a muse rule to let thinkers think.

"It could be the following," Phoebe said, opening her eyes. But Harold was gone. She looked this way and that and finally found him crawling up the side of her jewelry box.

"Are you off?" she said.

"No, no! Just doing my walking meditation. Shall I return to the sill?"

"Please! Otherwise I have to scrunch down. I don't think well scrunched!"

They resumed their original positions, though this took Phoebe one second and Harold a full minute.

"Here's what I think," Phoebe began. "I have one brain with a lot of brain cells. Agreed?"

"Agreed!" Harold agreed enthusiastically.

"Now, what is a brain like? Probably you will say a computer, because everybody does."

"I have never likened the brain to a computer—"

"Never mind. Grown ups always do. But I think the brain is like a jungle full of animals. Now, when they are all going about their own business, many things happen. We have thoughts about warm buns for breakfast, maybe we have a worry about the paper we have to write about the barge canals of England, maybe we think about that new CD we so desperately want. In short, we have a common mind full of common thoughts. Are you following?"

"Yes! I know that mind."

"Exactly. Now, in order for the brain to write, all the animals must come together and form a community. The lions and dolphins must get on the same page."

"Dolphins?"

214

"A little literary license, please! But if the lemurs and skinks—"

"Skinks?"

"An interesting animal I saw on our summer vacation in Hawaii."

"All right."

"If the lemurs and skinks are muttering about the all-girl band novel, even though they are far in the back of the circle and hardly audible at all, they will be causing a kind of—" Phoebe paused, searching for the right word.

"Upsetness?" Harold offered.

"Pandemonium! A little pandemonium. Which prevents the group from concentrating on the laundry story, even though the majority of the animals have agreed on the story."

"With the skinks carrying on so."

"And the lemurs! So that is my analogy. One has to really choose what one is writing, because if one says, 'I can write both,' that's somehow like letting skinks and lemurs loose, which produces upsetness and pandemonium."

Harold clapped. "I believe I can visualize that perfectly. The fire around which the animals gather, the exotic birds—"

"All right, Harold. I'm done with my analogy. Now—I must choose!"

Phoebe squizzled up her face something awful. It was a dramatic gesture considerably for Harold's benefit, and in fact after about three seconds she could feel a headache coming on.

"That won't do!" she exclaimed. "Choosing isn't like wrestling, after all!"

They were silent for a while as Phoebe tried to determine what choosing WAS like. Harold cleared his throat.

"Yes?" Phoebe grumped.

"You may take this to be a bit rude—"

"Well, then don't say it! For I imagine that you know perfectly well that what you are about to say WILL be rude, so why say it?"

"Yes, yes, I admit that. But muses do have certain duties after all, and one is to point out this and that. I am pointing out the following: that in the time it is taking you to choose, you could have your laundry on the line already."

"Well!" Phoebe huffed. She had the urge to roll up the magazine beside her and give Harold one great thwump. "That was not just rude, that was idiotic! That's like saying—" Here she paused and thought hard, because only the right analogy would sting Harold sufficiently. "That's like saying you could already be on the moon, if you didn't waste so much time building your rocket! I mean, choosing is a PROCESS, and processes take time!"

"Of course, of course," Harold agreed. "But it isn't quite so much like building a rocket. I mean, laundry or island. Not to be small-minded about it, my dear, but it's JUST a choice, not literal interstellar engineering."

Phoebe's feelings were bitterly hurt. "Well," she said, a tear or two angling to venture forth from her tear ducts. "So you think I'm just a slacker. A slouch. A sloth. That I am just AVOIDING writing. That I am just talking the talk and not walking the walk. Well. I am quite sure that you are a very bad muse bearing very bad news and I wish you would crawl away and evaporate."

"Now, now—"

"Go away, you mean little spider!"

Harold waited for Phoebe to recover but she looked greener and purpler by the second, so finally he trotted off. Phoebe threw herself on her bed, which wasn't so much of a throw that she was likely to injure herself, and snuffled for fifteen minutes. Then she sat straight up.

"Well. There's something to what that spider said!" she said to Lexington, the closest cat. "But he was also wrong. Right and wrong both, I say! Choosing IS a process. But perhaps I lingered and dawdled a bit too long. Maybe I WAS delaying, not really wanting to start anything. Plus, I'm not sure the laundry story was really my cup of tea. I think I liked the SMELL of it more than the story. Because I could smell that fresh laundry, which was really very delicious. So I suppose that I wanted to write the novel all along. But maybe I was secretly saying to myself, 'What thirteen-year-old girl writes a novel?' I fear that I WAS saying such a thing, so familiar does that question sound! Well! Who knew? I had NO IDEA I was doubting myself!"

This realization was really breathtaking and Phoebe had to catch her breath. She never consciously thought that there was anything she couldn't do. To learn that she had some doubts about her ability to write a novel staggered her.

"Well, I'll be the skink's pajamas!" she exclaimed. "On to the novel immediately! I will eat late! I will write and write! Where are my pen and pad!"

She was indeed talking in exclamation points, which made Harold smile. On the ceiling, quite visible if you were looking that way, Harold waited another few seconds to see if Phoebe would open her pad. When she did, he trundled off, stopping only to nibble a red ant appetizer.

LESSON 33

If you won't choose, you can't create.

CHAPTER 34

Phoebe's Novel Gets Under Way

The following Saturday morning the forces of nature, her genetic makeup, the hidden influences of muses, and whatever else was stewing in the pot of her personal creativity caused Phoebe to really start her novel.

She felt suffused with a new feeling. Previously she had liked the general idea of writing a novel and the specific idea of her all-girl band story. She relished the idea of being an author, of seeing her book in shops, of catching a glimpse of her likeness on the back cover. She also quite enjoyed the actual writing, though not when it wasn't going well—which, it turned out, was disappointingly often. All in all, she would have said that she had been working on her novel for some weeks and had made a "fair start." This Saturday morning she knew better. That had all been preamble.

Today something was flowing in her with the intensity of an ice-white river powered by glacial melt. She felt cold, not hot, and distracted, not focused. It was a feeling the very opposite of what she supposed "really creating" must feel like. Yet she understood why this was so. She was distracted because plot lines were zipping by like asteroids past a starship, whizzing by as she sorted possibilities and made decisions.

How did the band get to the island? Why had they brought acoustic guitars with them if they only played electric? Who were they? Were they more like the Go-Gos, the B-52s, or the Bangles, three ancient all-girl bands about which Phoebe knew everything. What threats would she put in their way? Would the dangers be self-inflicted, arising out of personality conflicts—everyone envying the lead singer, say, who, it turned out, could not only hit the high notes but make fire—or would they arrive from the outside—volcanic eruptions, pirates, poisonous lizards?

These thoughts were zooming by even as she wrote the opening scenes, having to do with the band's dynamite last concert on their doomed cruise ship. She had her laptop booted up and she was typing furiously. "*Fame* meets *Titanic*," Phoebe said to herself as she pounded away. Her thoughts leaped ahead as she made plot decisions, invented villains, created the ferns and bamboo groves of her island, foreshadowed the last several plot twists without which her thriller wouldn't thrill. Phoebe was humming.

She didn't notice the bevy of muses present. The frog and the bee were playing cribbage in a corner, occasionally exclaiming things like "Fifteen for two, fifteen for four, and a pair for six!" Melanie Caterpillar was nibbling on a leaf she must have brought in from outside, there being no flora in Phoebe's room. Harold Spider was reading a musty old book that Phoebe had purchased at a library book sale, a collection of travel anecdotes by famous writers. Other muses came and went, some leaving to do their laundry.

Phoebe had been writing for almost an hour when a serious doubt crossed her mind. "This is mere ENTERTAINMENT!" she heard herself exclaim. "Where's the depth? Where's the BEEF?"

The muses stopped what they were doing. This was the kind of thought that could stop a novel for a month or a lifetime. They held their breath. Suddenly Phoebe laughed. "But a young girl is entitled to write one entertainment. I can write *Crime and Punishment* when I'm fifteen or sixteen!"

The muses sighed. Crisis over!

Fifteen minutes later, after she'd mangled a sentence, Phoebe exclaimed, "What pitiful prose!" Her faced turned pruney. She reread her morning's work and wanted to vomit. "Bad writing everywhere!" she cried. "No power! No resonance! I have been BORING!"

This was worse than the previous crisis. The muses waited nervously. But Phoebe laughed her accusation away. "Get real, girl! Everybody knows that writing is rewriting!"

Phoebe resumed her wild typing. The phone rang. The muses would have liked her not to answer, but they understood that for most people not answering the phone was quite impossible. Phoebe grabbed her portable phone.

"Hello!"

It was Wanda. "Will you come shopping with me at the mall? I have to buy—"

"Sorry! I'm working on my novel today! See you on Monday!"

She hung up unceremoniously.

A minute later the phone rang again. This time it was her writer friend Abigail, a real grown-up writer.

"We're taking the boys on a picnic to Zaca Creek. Want to come? I made a pasta salad with green olives and pine nuts—"

"Sorry! I'm working on my novel today!"

There was a pause on the other end. "So am I! What was I thinking? Who has time to picnic?"

Phoebe felt a pang of guilt for having ruined the picnic for Rory and Raymond, Abigail's sons. But of course that wasn't her fault. People like Abigail had to decide for themselves when they would write, when they would picnic, and whether their children mattered. Phoebe returned to her furious clacking.

The phone rang again. Phoebe shook her head and almost didn't answer it. But what if it happened to be a literary agent who, by magic, had become aware of Phoebe's novel and its greatness? She couldn't risk turning such a call over to voice mail. She hit the talk button.

"Hello!" cried a familiar voice. "This is Margot. Remember me? I'm the girl who was fired from dance class. The girl you wouldn't join in the fountain. I'm out of the hospital now and I'd like to come by. I have quite a story to tell you!"

"I'm sorry, Margot. I'm working on my novel today and every other spare minute I've got."

"I could help you with your novel! Let me come over. We could collaborate!"

"I'm sorry, Margot. Why don't you write your own book?"

"Thanks for nothing!"

Margot hung up. Phoebe shook her head. She didn't understand Margot's mania, for which the poor girl had been hospitalized. Her own mild mania was clearly a cat of another stripe, just passion and excitement raring to go. Without giving Margot another thought, she returned to the cruise ship ballroom where her all-girl band was playing its last killer concert.

Unbelievably, the phone rang a fourth time. This time Phoebe answered angrily.

"Hello!"

"Is Mr. or Mrs. Barlow there?"

"They're not! Can I take a message?"

"Maybe you're able to make decisions about refinancing your home mortgage? Because rates have never been lower—"

"Mortgage rates were MUCH lower right after World War II," Phoebe interrupted, as she had done a paper on the subject for history class. "And no, I am not able to make such decisions. And I really must go!"

Phoebe tried returning to her novel. But suddenly nothing was there. She squinched her face up and tried to picture her ballroom scene. Suddenly Harold Spider sneezed.

"Musty book I'm reading," Harold Spider apologized. "Mold."

"Thank you very much!" Phoebe cried. "I'm trying to concentrate! What kind of muse are you, sneezing when a person is thinking!"

"Sorry," Harold Spider said. He sneezed three more times and apologized three more times.

"Wonderful!" Phoebe cried. "My concentration is broken. My spirit is broken. Plus I'm hungry!"

"A little sneezing—" Harold Spider began.

Phoebe crumpled onto her beanbag chair. She sat there, arms and legs akimbo, for several seconds. Then she popped up. "Well!" she exclaimed. "I had a glorious start to this novel-writing day and a very ignominious finish. Should I call this a good day or a bad day?"

The muses waited anxiously.

"I'll make myself a snack and then decide," Phoebe said. She had a sudden thought. "Creating is one emotional roller coaster! Who knew?"

No one—not muse, man, or beast—could have said whether Phoebe would return to her novel that day, that week, or ever. A black cloud scudded over Gold Strike but the sun beat it away. Another black cloud scudded by. So it would be until the end of time. Novels would commence; some would be finished; many would not. Phoebe made herself a snack plate of baby carrots and golden raisins and listened to loud music through her headphones.

LESSON 34

There will always be interruptions. How will you handle them?

CHAPTER 35

The Writer of Qualities

T he Gold Strike Writers Club, a branch of the California Writers Club, met once a month at Sylvan's Restaurant for lunch and a guest speaker. Usually about thirty people attended, most of them of retirement age. That number swelled to forty or fifty on special occasions, for instance when awards were handed out to winners of the club's competition for middle-school writers or when a famous guest speaker came to talk. Phoebe had learned about the club from a flyer posted outside the English office, inviting students to submit a short story or a poem to the competition. Phoebe was toying with the idea.

Mildly curious about the club, she attended two meetings. At one the guest speaker discussed foreign reporting; a second featured a mystery writer whose mysteries were organized around body parts (*A Head for Murder*, *The Eyes Have It*, *Dead by a Hair*, and so on). Each time she bought a raffle ticket and won, once winning a potted plant (the only prize left on the table) and the second time choosing a book of poetry self-published by a club member, who inscribed the book on the spot.

A celebrity guest was coming to speak at the April meeting and Phoebe decided to attend. The main problem was the lunch choice. The first time Phoebe had ribs, which were very good but a tad too messy for simultaneous eating-and-socializing. The second time she had broiled salmon, which she discovered could be prepared as appetizingly as dry wall. What to eat? Finally she decided on the Caesar Chicken Salad, half-relishing the idea of a chopped-up Roman emperor. She mailed off her parents' check and her lunch choice and waited expectantly for the Saturday in question.

Veronica Blake, the celebrity guest, had written six or seven novels. Phoebe had read three of them. They were very beautiful, very lively, very deep. From the first sentence you knew that you were reading a novel that was going to take you somewhere. The author had control of her ideas and control of her details. Phoebe loved her ethics, or maybe it was her philosophy.

The first one she read was about a dispute in Greenland over the ownership of some reindeer. The second was set in the Holy Land and focused on a love affair between a Palestinian woman and a Jewish man. The third was set in Boston and had to do with a white-collar crime that everyone refused to take seriously, juxtaposed against the life sentence meted out to an Angolan for smuggling drugs.

Phoebe arrived early at Sylvan's Restaurant on the Saturday when Veronica Blake was to speak. She arrived even before the club had set up its ticket-taker table, book table, or raffle table. Several people were in the room where the event was to be held, four or five of them together at a meeting of some sort, the remaining person at a separate table.

The lone individual was Veronica Blake, who was glancing at a sheet of paper. Phoebe sidled over, using as an excuse the photographs on the wall behind Veronica's chair, which photographs Phoebe began studiously examining.

Veronica looked up and smiled. Phoebe smiled back.

"Your speech?" Phoebe said, nodding at the piece of paper.

"No," Veronica replied pleasantly. "A reminder list of the me I would like to be."

"Really? You need to remind yourself?"

"Absolutely! Everybody does."

"You look at it often?"

"I 'cast furtive glances' at it, as a romance writer would say. The list is very long and daunting. It's hard and even a little painful to look at it too directly. Like looking at the sun. You know not to look at the sun directly, but you also know that you need it, yes?"

"Yes!"

A question sprang to Phoebe's mind. But she was shy about asking it. Veronica smiled, which permitted Phoebe to plunge ahead.

"Do you plot your novels?" Phoebe asked. "Or do you just write them?"

"I plot," Veronica Blake replied. "I get more immediate pleasure if I just start, write the scenes that come to me, jot down fragments of dialogue, and let the novel come to life that way. But I no longer trust that method, even though it feels natural. What I now prefer to do is to take a lot of time trying to understand my novel before I write too much of it. I call that 'figuring out what's at stake.' It's sort of like plotting and sort of like arriving at a theme, but it's different from either.

"Sometimes it takes three or four months to arrive at this thing I'm talking about—knowing what's at stake—because that whole time I have to push aside too-easy solutions, so as to make room for the right solution. In a way it's more like demolition than creation, because I have to demolish my first, often wrong-headed ideas of what to do with the novel. I have to expose the real reason for writing it. This process I'm describing requires exactly the qualities on my list: the discipline, the energy, the thoughtfulness, and so on. Does that make sense? Have I explained myself clearly?"

"I think you've explained yourself beautifully!" Phoebe replied. "I just don't know enough about writing novels to really appreciate what you're saying. I wish I did! I wish I'd written so many bad novels that I could really use your advice! My guess is that what you're saying will come back to me in six or seven years, after I've made a mess of several novels. Then I'll go, 'O-ho! That's what Veronica Blake meant!'"

Veronica Blake smiled. "You may be right! I certainly had to write those bad first novels!"

People were arriving. It was clear that a large group was coming. A woman diffidently approached Veronica. Assigned to introduce her, she was very nervous and wondered if she could go over her introduction. Phoebe excused herself and found a seat for lunch.

After lunch and a painfully long and halting introduction, which Veronica Blake sat through graciously, a smile of encouragement never far from her lips, the guest of honor rose to speak. She took her place at the podium and allowed the crowd to settle.

"Many people dream of writing a novel and a sizable number of them start one," she began. "Typically it doesn't go very well and after not too long they find themselves saying, 'I don't have what it takes.' Anxious and discouraged, they fail to ask the question that naturally arises from this thought—namely, 'What WOULD it take?'"

She paused and took a sip of water.

"They don't ask the question because they fear the answer. They fear they may learn that they really don't have what it takes. This result, they imagine, would be worse than saying 'I don't have what it takes' and throwing in the towel. They're wrong! Not creating is worse than trying and possibly failing."

She glanced around the room.

"What they would discover, if they asked themselves that natural question, is that what it takes to write a good novel is very simple to say and even simple to accomplish, in a certain sense. It doesn't take talent, which is a word I would never think of using. What it takes is resolve, discipline, courage—in short, qualities of character."

She paused for emphasis.

"That's the long and the short of it. If I wanted to do something which I currently believe I couldn't do, like become a bassoonist or learn physics, first I would have to quiet the voice in me that wants to say, 'You have no talent for that!' and remind myself of what I know to be true, that I might have a chance to do either of those things if I applied myself. Through the application of the best qualities in my character I could do just about anything, as can you."

Veronica Blake paused again. Phoebe thought that Veronica had caught her eye and smiled, but all she was sure of was the smile. After another sip of water Veronica continued.

She spoke for forty-five minutes. It was an inspirational talk but also rather somber and dark. She kept demanding things of her audience, that they write every day, that they write first thing each morning, that they commit to a piece of writing and write it all the way through without abandoning it. At the end of her talk she received a very nice round of applause. But it wasn't the hearty applause she would have gotten if she'd just told funny anecdotes and asked less of them.

Phoebe understood. This was a quality speech from a person who loved good qualities. Phoebe wondered where she might get her hands on Veronica Blake's list. Then she laughed. Of course she already knew what those qualities were—everybody knew what they were. You didn't need to steal Veronica's list. You just needed to heroically listen to your own conscience. Phoebe finished her Sprite and left the restaurant just as the raffle was beginning.

LESSON 35

Become more creative by improving your character.

CHAPTER 36

Phoebe's Novel Blooms in the Silence

Saturday morning was so quiet that you could hear stars being born. A silence deeper than a monastery garden's enveloped Gold Strike and the canyons and valleys from the state capital to Platinum Lake. It was just an ordinary May day, no different from a million other May days, but altogether hushed.

Mrs. Snyder in Blue Bluff, frightened by the silence, mistook the reflection of the sun on some scudding clouds for an alien spacecraft and reported a UFO. Mr. McFeeny in Mine Shaft, transformed by the silence, dropped his lawsuit against his neighbor, with whom he had been fighting about the trimming of a weeping willow. Mr. Redspan went fishing. Two people in Palestine fell in love. In Paris, where it was very chilly but equally quiet, a baker decided to bake baguettes in the old way. The aroma wafting from his oven made women in the rue Mouffetard weep.

Phoebe sensed that a silence this deep could precipitate any-thing. It could make you color your hair red, go mad, jump into the shower, or start a new novel. The silence was golden, dangerous, pregnant, provocative. When you turned on the television you had to turn it right off again, because the sounds the television characters made were like little explosions. *Boom! Bam!* The same with voices on the radio, the ring of the telephone, the six notes that the doorbell chimed. *Bam! Boom!* Even the tiniest sound, like Melanie Caterpillar crossing the carpet, shook you like a jet breaking the sound barrier.

Suddenly it struck Phoebe: "Why do I need a round island?"

She had been supposing that the island upon which her all-girl band was stranded was round, for no other reason than islands that you pictured were always round, just like lemons were yellow and tangerines orange. Now Phoebe realized that a round island wasn't the only possibility and didn't really serve her novel. She had been stuck because of the roundness of her island, which roundness prevented certain adventures. Suddenly she came unstuck.

Her island was the wrong shape!

She had to research islands. Why hadn't that occurred to her before? She had given lots of thought to the shape of her plot but none to the shape of her island. What a strange lapse or blind spot. She got dressed all in a rush, said hello and goodbye to her parents, and stopped, as the library wasn't open yet, for a hot chocolate and an almond croissant at her favorite café. Then, at ten, she hurried off to begin her research.

She'd never had that much interest in islands. On a scale of one to ten, she would have rated her interest as a modest five or six. She hadn't read *Robinson Crusoe, Treasure Island*, or *Swiss Family Robinson*. Unlike her hunger for Paris, she had no hunger for Hawaii, the Bahamas, or Tahiti. She was a city girl at heart, indifferent to the glories of barrier reefs, secluded beaches, or azure bays. But her all-girl band needed the right island. Phoebe dove in.

Over the next few hours she researched a zillion islands: Socotra; the Turkish island of Bozcaada Adasi; the French island of Porquerolles; even mythical islands like Bingfield's Island, Luquebaralideaux, and Harmattan Rocks. Nantucket. Australia. Islands in Micronesia. Islands in the Black Sea. Famous Greek islands and unknown Greek islands. Islands no bigger than your thumb. Islands that were continents. Islands as long and thin as a licorice whip, L-shaped islands, U-shaped islands, even K-shaped and P-shaped islands.

Some were incredibly barren. Many were mere rocks with birds roosting. Some had black beaches and a couple had red beaches. The beaches! Rio's famous beach, bursting with bronzed bodies. A beautiful Hawaiian beach, palm trees fluttering. South Beach in Miami, perfectly still and empty as it awaited a hurricane. A beach in Thailand where they brought you whole pineapples as you reclined.

Then, in a magazine, she encountered the wildest thing. You could buy islands! There were even island brokers, real estate agents who specialized in basalt baubles and sea-wrapped dreams. This news made her head spin. That could be part of the plot!—not that she knew how it might fit. Her mind raced, creating different plots, some which no longer included her all-girl band at all. Her novel was vanishing in favor of new novels careening into existence simply because she had learned a fact. How upsetting! It was really incredible, when you thought about it, that your plot could be completely overthrown by one random bit of news.

"Get a grip!" she heard herself cry. The librarian flung her a dirty look.

Fighting off a torrent of exciting new possibilities, she returned with a vengeance to her current plot. She had been stuck for some time with a problem in logic. The girls see a light in the distance and believe it to be a ship. Only days later do they discover that the light came from a beachside campfire and signaled the presence of other island dwellers. But how could they have confused a shore fire with a ship light? This plot problem had stumped Phoebe for two whole weeks.

Then it struck her: the shape of her island! It could be L-shaped! Then, naturally, the girls might think that the light was out at sea, if a fire had been built at the tip of the L. It would be an optical illusion based on the false assumption that their island was round, which nicely dovetailed with other false assumptions Phoebe wanted to introduce, like Mercedes supposing that Flo wasn't brave simply because she couldn't swim (Phoebe didn't swim) and Jacqueline supposing that Lily didn't matter simply because she was short (Phoebe being not that tall).

This was SO pleasing. It was perfect. She had a very grown-up theme—false assumptions—and a nice plot twist to drive her theme home. What more could a girl want! "This is the life!" Phoebe exclaimed out loud. "Summer vacation I'll be here eight hours a day!"

"Quiet!" the librarian scolded.

"Or in a café!" Phoebe whispered. "Where you can cry out occasionally!"

Several muses had arrived. Harold Spider strolled across her pile of island magazines. The frog and the bee broke out a deck of cards and a cribbage board. Phoebe smiled. Maybe this wasn't real life. Or maybe it was a life you could have if you believed you could have it. You would need Veronica Blake's list of qualities, not as a list on paper but as the metal of your life. You might need to learn how to cook your meals in a toaster oven, because you might be very poor. You might need to learn how to barter for movie tickets, sing for your supper, live on air. Still, what life was better?

You could spend time in libraries. You could travel the whole world just by dreaming. You could create fine scrapes and get your characters out of them. You could say deep things about the human condition. Then, after a few hours of that, you could go for a walk and get an ice cream. Which was exactly what was now called for: a nice pralines-and-cream on a sugar cone. Phoebe gathered up her novel-in-progress, scattering several muses and flipping the frog completely upside down.

"Don't touch my cards!" the frog cried at the bee.

"I wouldn't DREAM of touching your cards!" the bee screamed back. "Like a bee can't beat a frog fairly!"

"What IS that horrible racket!" the librarian exclaimed, jumping to her feet.

Phoebe rushed out of the library. Outside, the air smelled sweet. The sun shone. Best of all, it was still the weekend! It was, all things considered, heavenly.

LESSON 36

Creating is Heaven. Or close enough.

Index

Other Works by the Author

Many of the ideas I discussed in *A Writer's Space* are elaborated in my other books, among them:

Ten Zen Seconds
Creativity for Life
The Van Gogh Blues
Fearless Creating
Coaching the Artist Within
The Creativity Book

Toxic Criticism
Affirmations for Artists
A Writer's Paris
A Writer's San Francisco
Creative Recovery

About the Author

Eric Maisel, Ph.D., is the author of more than thirty books. He holds bachelor's degrees in philosophy and psychology, master's degrees in creative writing and counseling, and a doctorate in counseling psychology. He is a California licensed marriage and family therapist, a creativity coach and trainer of creativity coaches, a columnist for *Art Calendar Magazine*, provides regular segments for *Art of the Song Creativity Radio*, and hosts two shows on the Personal Life Media Network, *The Joy of Living Creatively* and *Your Purpose-Centered Life*. He lives in San Francisco.

Dr. Maisel is widely regarded as America's foremost creativity coach and has taught thousands of creative and performing artists how to meet the challenges of the creative life.

Dr. Maisel has presented the keynote address at the Pikes Peak Writers Conference, the Jack London Writers Conference, the William Saroyan Writers Conference, the Oklahoma Federation of Writers Conference, and scores of other venues, including repeat appearances at the Romance Writers of America annual conference and the Paris Writers Workshop. Dr. Maisel also produces e-books available at his Web site, including the e-book *Becoming a Creativity Coach*, which details the art and practice of creativity coaching. You can visit Dr. Maisel at *www.ericmaisel.com* or contact him at *ericmaisel@hotmail.com.*